POCKET SPOTTERS
SEASHELLS

Theodore Roland-Entwistle

CHRYSALIS CHILDREN'S BOOKS

Shell Collector's Code

1 Always go collecting with a friend, and always tell an adult where you are going.

2 Keep a careful eye on the tide, and make sure you can reach safety if the tide starts to come in. Remember that beaches can be dangerous places as well as pleasant ones.

3 Ask permission before crossing private property to reach a beach or going on a private landing stage.

4 Don't walk under overhanging cliffs.

5 Avoid doing any damage to the environment, or harming any living creature you come across.

6 Take your litter home with you.

This edition published in 2004 by
Chrysalis Children's Books, an imprint of Chrysalis Books
Group PLC, The Chrysalis Building, Bramley Road,
London, W10 6SP

Copyright © Chrysalis Books Group PLC

Author Theodore Roland-Entwistle
Senior editor Rasha Elsaeed
Editorial director Honor Head
Art director Sophie Wilkins
Designers James Lawrence, Victoria Furbisher and Gemma Cooper
Cover designer Ed Simkins
Photograhy R. Tucker Abbott, David Parmiter
Headbands Antonia Philips
Activities illustrator Richard Coombes

British Library Cataloguing in Publication Data for this book is available from the British Library.

ISBN 1 903954 89 4

Printed and bound in Malaysia

Useful internet websites

http://www.uksafari.com/ marine.htm
Wildlife to look out for on UK beaches, including sea shells.

http://www.gastropods.com/
If you know the name of a shell, look it up to see a picture.

http://www.somali.asso.fr/ clemam/taxis.php
If you've got a shell, look for its picture to find out what it is.

Contents

Introduction

You can find seashells on just about every seashore of Europe. These hard, colourful cases were (and often still are) the homes of living animals, relatives of the snails that you find in your garden. They belong to a group called the molluscs. You can learn a lot about molluscs and their life, by collecting their shells and studying live specimens in temporary aquariums.

There are about 60,000 different kinds of seashells world-wide, but you are unlikely to find more than a few hundred even if you search every beach in Europe.

This book shows and describes those you are most likely to find because they live in shallow water, not far from the shore, and are the most common.

Some molluscs live in warm water, others in colder water. Biologists have divided the seas around western Europe into four provinces, according to average sea temperature of those areas. Some species can be found in more than one province, because they can tolerate a wide range of sea temperatures or have adapted to local conditions.

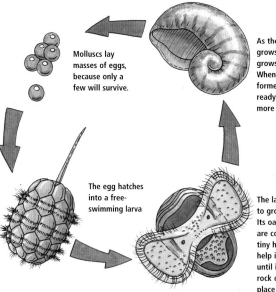

Molluscs lay masses of eggs, because only a few will survive.

As the mollusc grows, its shell grows with it. When it is fully formed, it will be ready to produce more eggs.

The egg hatches into a free-swimming larva

The larva begins to grow a shell. Its oar-like flaps are covered with tiny hairs, which help it to swim until it finds a rock or other place to settle.

Life of a Seashell

Different kinds or species of molluscs reproduce themselves in different ways. Some molluscs leave their eggs to float freely in the water. Others hide them in the sand, in a living sponge, or in a fold of their own bodies. Some species of mollusc have separate males and females (as humans do). In other molluscs the same animal is both male and female.

Arctic Province: very few species live here. The sea temperature ranges from 0° to 5° Centigrade.

Boreal Province: the sea temperature ranges from 5° to 10°C.

Celtic Province: the sea temperature ranges from 10° to 15°C.

Lusitanian Province: this includes the Mediterranean and Black Seas. The sea temperature ranges from 15° to 20°C.

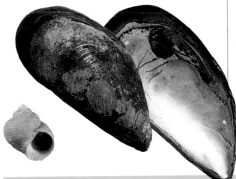

How to use this book

To identify a shell you do not recognize – for example the two shown left – follow these steps.

1 **Decide what kind of beach you are on.** Does it have rocky pools or sand or mud flats? Is it an estuary or are you looking at a bit of beach that is covered at high tide? Each type has a different picture band (see below).

2 **Decide what sort of mollusc you have found.** Is it a gastropod or a bivalve? See pages 6 and 7 if you don't know the difference.

3 **Look through the pages of shells** of this type and heading. The photo and information given for each mollusc will help you to identify it. You will find the gastropod shell is a Northern Rough Periwinkle – it's on page 14.

4 **If you can't find the shell**, look through the pages for other kinds of shore. Some shores are part sandy, part rocky for example. They may contain both kinds of shell. Again a shell from a nearby sandy beach might have been carried by the tide to a rocky beach. You will find the bivalve shell is a Blue Mussel, and it is shown on page 20.

5 **If you still can't find the shell**, you may have to look in a larger field guide (see page 78 for some suggestions). You may have picked up one that has been washed in from deep water or something that is very rare!

Habitat Picture Bands

Each habitat (type of beach) has a different picture band at the top of the page. These are shown below.

Rocky Pools and Shores

Sand or Mud Flats

Estuaries and Lagoons

Intertidal Rocks and Sand

Wood and Rock Borers

Kinds of shells

Biologists divide molluscs into seven groups, called classes, but only some of them count as seashells.

BIVALVES have two shells, or valves, hinged together. They include clams, oysters, and scallops.

GASTROPODS have a single shell. They include snails, periwinkles, whelks, and conches. Most have a coiled shell, although some (like limpets and slipper-shells) have a cap-shaped shell.

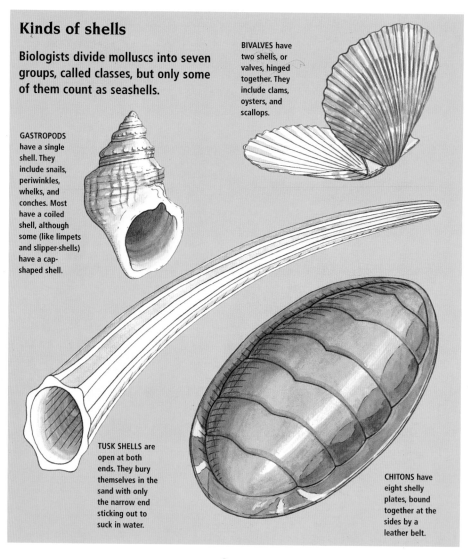

TUSK SHELLS are open at both ends. They bury themselves in the sand with only the narrow end sticking out to suck in water.

CHITONS have eight shelly plates, bound together at the sides by a leather belt.

Parts of a shell

This is a gastropod shell. The shape of the different sections, the colour, and their overall size will help you to identify gastropods.

The pointed part of the shell is called the spire. It was the first bit to be formed.

As the gastropod grew, it added a new whorl to the shell and moved into it. The number of whorls show how old the shell is.

The shell formed around this solid central pillar.

These ridges are called spiral cords.

The outer lip of the body whorl gets thicker as the gastropod gets older.

These ridges are called axial bands.

The largest section is called the body whorl. It is where the gastropod last lived.

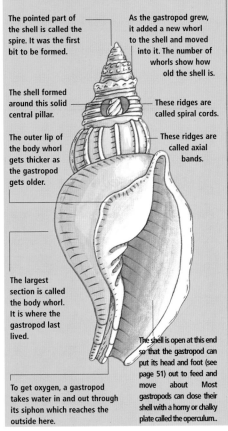

The shell is open at this end so that the gastropod can put its head and foot (see page 51) out to feed and move about Most gastropods can close their shell with a horny or chalky plate called the operculum..

To get oxygen, a gastropod takes water in and out through its siphon which reaches the outside here.

This is one half of a bivalve shell. The shape of the scars and the number of hinge teeth help to identify bivalves.

The hinge teeth allow the two valves to open and close.

The ligament holds the two valves of the mollusc together.

These scars show where the bivalve's adductor muscles gripped the shell. It used these muscles to keep the two halves closed.

The beak is the first bit of the shell to be formed.

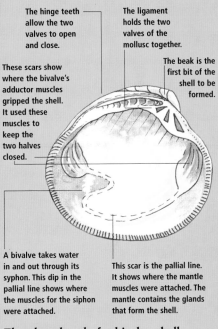

A bivalve takes water in and out through its syphon. This dip in the pallial line shows where the muscles for the siphon were attached.

This scar is the pallial line. It shows where the mantle muscles were attached. The mantle contains the glands that form the shell.

The closed end of a bivalve shell

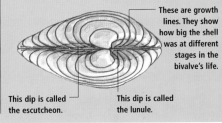

These are growth lines. They show how big the shell was at different stages in the bivalve's life.

This dip is called the escutcheon.

This dip is called the lunule.

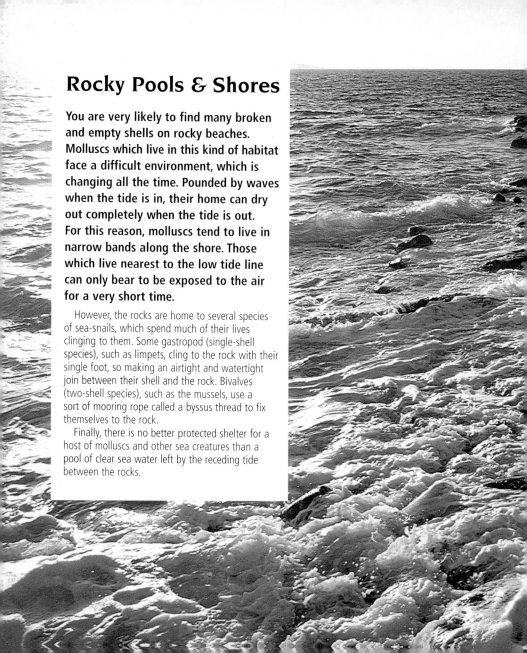

Rocky Pools & Shores

You are very likely to find many broken and empty shells on rocky beaches. Molluscs which live in this kind of habitat face a difficult environment, which is changing all the time. Pounded by waves when the tide is in, their home can dry out completely when the tide is out. For this reason, molluscs tend to live in narrow bands along the shore. Those which live nearest to the low tide line can only bear to be exposed to the air for a very short time.

However, the rocks are home to several species of sea-snails, which spend much of their lives clinging to them. Some gastropod (single-shell species), such as limpets, cling to the rock with their single foot, so making an airtight and watertight join between their shell and the rock. Bivalves (two-shell species), such as the mussels, use a sort of mooring rope called a byssus thread to fix themselves to the rock.

Finally, there is no better protected shelter for a host of molluscs and other sea creatures than a pool of clear sea water left by the receding tide between the rocks.

European Ormer

The ear-like shape of this sea-snail gives it its name of ormer, which comes from a French phrase meaning 'ear of the sea'. Its shell is rough, and a dark reddish-brown or mottled green outside. There are nine or ten open holes. The inside of the shell is bright, iridescent and very pearly. Its range is from the Channel Islands south to the Mediterranean.

Ormer family
About 6.5 cm long – Provinces: Celtic, Lusitanian
Named by Linnaeus in 1758

Blue-rayed Limpet

You will find this tiny limpet clinging not to rocks but to kelp weed. It is cap-shaped and horn-coloured. When young it is smooth and almost translucent, with narrow, bright blue rays. Older shells are thicker and may have lost the blue rays. The position of the apex of the shell varies with age and the surface on which the snail grows. It breeds in winter and spring, and is common along the very low tide line from Norway to Portugal.

Limpet family
About 0.5 cm long
Provinces:
Boreal, Celtic, Lusitanian
Named by
Linnaeus in 1758

Graecian Keyhole Limpet

This keyhole limpet has an oval shell, a little narrower towards the front end. It has numerous radiating ribs, alternately wide and narrow. Concentric threads cross the ribs to form small square pits. The colour is a dull yellow-brown, often with darker brown marks. The animal pushes the edge of its mantle through the keyhole to form a short siphon. It feeds on sponges. It is moderately common on subtidal rocks, from the southern coasts of the British Isles to the Mediterranean.

Keyhole Limpet family
About 2 cm long
Provinces:
Celtic, Lusitanian
Named by
Linnaeus in 1758

Common European Limpet

This limpet is one of the most characteristic sea-snails of the rocky shores. It has a solid oval shell, with many irregular tiny ribs. The outside colour varies from whitish to yellowish, sometimes streaked with dark brown. It can be found in large numbers at low tide, clinging to rocks from Norway to the Mediterranean. When covered by water it moves about in search of food. It is edible.

Limpet family – About 5 cm long
Provinces: Boreal, Celtic, Lusitanian
Named by Linnaeus in 1758

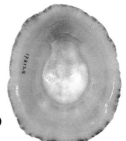 

European China Limpet

A longer, flatter shell marks the difference between this limpet and the Common European Limpet. Its shell has strong, sharp ribs, giving it a wavy edge. The inside of the shell is white, like porcelain, with a pale-orange mark in it. The apex is toward the front of the shell. The snail, whose body is cream or yellow, is common on rough, exposed coasts from southern Britain to southern France.

Limpet family
About 4 cm long
Province: Celtic
Named by Röding in 1798

Rustic Limpet

Commonly found between the high and low tide lines, the Rustic Limpet ranges from south-western France to the Adriatic Sea. It has a small, solid oval shell, which is cone-shaped. Its shell has many fine, uneven ribs. The outside varies in colour from pale yellowish-brown to grey, often with black marks on the ribs. The inside has broad brown or black rays on a silvery background.

Limpet family
About 2.5 cm long
Provinces: Celtic, Lusitanian
Named by Linnaeus in 1758

Rayed Mediterranean Limpet

Rocks on the mid-shore are home for this common southern European species, which also occurs in the Azores and the Canary Islands. It has a thin, depressed shell, with six or seven broadly rounded main ribs and many secondary ribs. The outer surface is whitish or buff.

Limpet family
About 5 cm long
Province: Lusitanian
Named by Linnaeus in 1758

Lined Monodont

A shell of the middle shore, the Lined Monodont has the popular name of Thick Topshell, because its shell is large, heavy and globular. The surface varies from smoothish to rough, with low spiral ridges. Its colour is dark grey mottled with brown. The snail itself is greyish-green. It is fairly common in rock pools from the southern British Isles to Portugal, feeding in seaweed and other vegetable matter.

Topshell family
About 3 cm long
Provinces: Celtic, Lusitanian
Named by da Costa in 1778

Turbinate Monodont

You can find this largish topshell in shallow rocky areas from Portugal to the Mediterranean and the Canary Islands. It has a thick-walled conical shell, which is basically white, tinged with greenish-grey, and with many square blotches of purplish-brown.

Topshell family
About 4 cm long
Province: Lusitanian
Named by Born in 1778

Articulate Monodont

This is a common seashore snail. Its range is from the Atlantic coast of France and Portugal into the Mediterranean. It has a solid shell, with a rounded spire and a rough surface. The colour is grey-green or dirty white, with spiral bands of alternating white and reddish-brown. Some specimens have spiral grooves.

Topshell family
About 2.5 cm long
Province: Lusitanian
Named by Lamarck in 1822

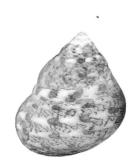

Magical Gibbula

The Magical Gibbula is one of the commonest species of topshell. It lives further down the shoreline than other topshells. It has a solid shell with ridged whorls, covered with lumps. The colour varies, with brown and red markings. Its range is from the southern British Isles south to the Mediterranean.

Topshell family
About 3 cm long
Provinces: Celtic, Lusitanian
Named by Linnaeus in 1758

Gualteri's Topshell

A polished, conical shell distinguishes this little sea-snail. Its shell is solid, yellowish-brown or olive in colour with some dark-brown markings. The inside of the aperture is smooth and pearly, sometimes purple. Its range is from Portugal south into the Mediterranean.

Topshell family
About 1 cm long
Province: Lusitanian
Named by
Philippi in 1848

Grey Topshell

Other names for this topshell are Silver Tommy or Ashen Gibbula. Its shell is solid and somewhat dome-shaped, with a blunt apex to the spire. It is yellowish in colour with broken, slanting streaks of brownish-purple. It is very common on the lower shore, among weeds and under stones. Its range is from Iceland to Portugal.

Topshell family
About 2 cm long – Provinces: Boreal, Celtic, Lusitanian
Named by Linnaeus in 1758

Flat Topshell

The other popular name for this topshell is Purple Top. The names are derived from its shape and colouring. It is also called the Umbilicate Gibbula. The shell is basically cream in colour, with speckles of reddish-brown. It is found higher up the shore than many other topshells. Its range is from the southern British Isles to the Mediterranean.

Topshell family
About 2 cm long – Provinces: Celtic, Lusitanian
Named by da Costa in 1778

Rocky Pools & Shores

Common Periwinkle

This is the largest periwinkle, and it is found in large numbers on rocks, in rock pools and on seaweed along the low tide line. It has a solid, globe-shaped shell, drab grey in colour, sometimes with fine spiral white streaks. Like all periwinkles, it is vegetarian. Its range is from Greenland through Norway to the Mediterranean. The Common Periwinkle is edible.

Periwinkle family – About 2.5 cm long

Provinces: Arctic, Boreal, Celtic, Lusitanian

Named by Linnaeus in 1758

Northern Yellow Periwinkle

Because its shell is flatter than other periwinkles, this snail is also called the Flat Winkle. It has a solid, globe-shaped shell, smooth on the outside. Most shells are a bright brownish-yellow or orange-yellow, but the colour may vary. It is a common rocky coast species, usually hidden under clumps of seaweed on which it lays its jellylike egg masses. Its range is from Norway to the Mediterranean.

Periwinkle family

About 1 cm long – Provinces: Boreal, Celtic, Lusitanian

Named by Linnaeus in 1758

Northern Rough Periwinkle

The Rough Periwinkle is fairly common, and is found on the upper part of rocky beaches, among the barnacles. Its range is from Norway to France. Its pointed shell has a smoothish surface. The colour ranges from orange to yellowish grey, with a darker pattern and a dark aperture. The females give birth to live young – complete with shells.

Periwinkle family

About 0.5 cm long – Provinces: Boreal, Celtic

Named by Olivi in 1792

European Chinese Hat

Also called the Chinaman's Hat, from its shape, the shell of this limpet has a circular base, with the apex in the centre. The colour is yellowish-white, and the snail itself is yellowish. It is common in shallow water on rocks and other shells from the British Isles south to Portugal.

Slipper Shell family
About 2.5 cm long
Provinces: Celtic, Lusitanian
Named by
Linnaeus in 1758

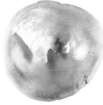

European White Slipper-shell

The broad shelf inside a slipper-shell protects this snail's digestive gland. The shell is solid, dull white to dirty grey on the outside, but pure white inside. The shelf is about half the length of the shell. The animal is commonly found on large dead shells. The species ranges from the Atlantic coast of France and Portugal to the Mediterranean. It is also called the Slipper Limpet.

Slipper-shell family
About 2.5 cm long
Provinces: Celtic, Lusitanian
Named by Lamarck in 1822

Flea Trivia

All trivias are shaped like cowrie shells, hence their general description as 'allied cowries'. The Flea Trivia's shell is rounded but elongated, glossy pinkish-brown in colour on the top surface, and whitish around the aperture. There are many fine ribs. This is an intertidal warm water species, found in the Mediterranean, the Azores and ranging north to Portugal.

Trivia family
About 7 mm long – Province: Lusitanian
Named by Link in 1807

Nun Trivia

This animal is much larger than the Flea Trivia. It has a similar-shaped, solid shell, coloured brownish-pink, with three darker spots on top. There are about twenty-eight strong ribs. The narrow aperture has about sixteen teeth on one side. It is moderately common along the low tide line from the British Isles to the Mediterranean.

Trivia family
About 2 cm long
Provinces:
Celtic, Lusitanian
Named by
da Costa in 1778

Purple Dye Murex

This snail was the main source of the Imperial Purple dye produced at Tyre (now in southern Lebanon) in ancient times. The Romans allowed only their nobles to wear cloth dyed in this colour. Its shell has a swollen body whorl, and a long, straight canal for the animal's siphon. There are two rows of short spines on each whorl. It is coloured yellowish-grey. The snail is carnivorous. It is mainly in The Mediterranean, but is also found off Portugal and West Africa.

Murex and Rock Shell family
About 6.5 cm long
Province: Lusitanian
Named by Linnaeus in 1758

Atlantic Dogwinkle

This snail is also called a Dog Whelk. It has a spindle-shaped shell with a pointed spire. Some specimens have smooth shells, others are sculptured. The colour is generally dull white, but may be tinged with yellow, orange or brown, occasionally with dark-brown spiral bands. The snail is very common along rocky coasts from Norway to northern Portugal. It feeds on mussels, making holes in their shells by secreting acid. It gives off a purple dye, which was once used as an indelible ink for marking laundry

Murex and Rock Shell family
About 4 cm long – Provinces: Boreal, Celtic, Lusitanian
Named by Linnaeus in 1758

Sting Winkle

The Sting Winkle, or Boring Whelk, is a pest found on oyster beds. It has a heavily sculptured shell with thick walls and a sharp spire. The colour is yellowish, often with brown bands. It is common just below the low tide line. In spring you may find its clusters of urn-shaped egg capsules. It ranges from the British Isles to the Mediterranean and the Azores. The similar but smoother Oyster Drill was accidentally introduced to England from America in the 1920s.

Murex and Rock Shell family
About 5 cm long – Provinces: Celtic, Lusitanian
Named by Linnaeus in 1758

Edwards' Dwarf Winkle

Despite its name, this small rock shell is not a periwinkle. It has a spindle-shaped, tan-coloured shell with six whorls. Each whorl has about sixteen rounded axial ribs, crossed by fine threads of a lighter tan. The siphonal canal is short. The snail is a shallow water, hard-bottom species common in the Mediterranean and on the Portuguese coast.

Murex and Rock Shell family
About 2 cm long
Province: Lusitanian
Named by Payraudeau in 1826

Spindle Dwarf Triton

Tritons get their names from the Ancient Greek sea god Triton, who used a conch shell as a horn. Triton shells look a bit like tiny conch shells. This mollusc's shell is spindle-shaped with six whorls. There are nine or ten rounded axial ribs, crossed by numerous spiral cords. The spire is pointed. The snail is moderately common in rocky shallow areas in the Mediterranean and western Europe.

Murex and Rock Shell family
About.2 cm long
Provinces: Lusitanian, Celtic
Named by Brocchi in 1814

Sharp Dwarf Winkle

The pointed spire gives this snail its name. Its small shell is heavily ornamented with eight to ten slanting axial ribs crossed by spiral threads. The colour varies from tan to orange-buff. The animal is red flecked with yellow. Its diet is thought to be small barnacles. It is common from the southern British Isles to the Mediterranean.

Murex and Rock Shell family
About 2 cm long
Provinces: Celtic, Lusitanian
Named by Lamarck in 1822

Crested Dwarf Triton

This snail has a slender, knobbly shell with a pointed spire. It is brown with two broad spiral yellowish bands. The longish siphonal canal is open throughout its length. The snail lives in intertidal rocky areas in the Mediterranean, and is found down the West African coast and also north to Portugal.

Murex and Rock Shell family
About 2.5 cm long
Province: Lusitanian
Named by Brocchi in 1814

Ebony Mitre

The Ebony Mitre, or Mitre Shell, is moderately common in rock pools in Portugal and the Mediterranean. The snail has a glossy blackish-brown shell, with a narrow tan band on the upper part of the last whorl. There are ten low, rounded ribs, and the outer lip of the aperture has tiny teeth on the inner edge. The snail is carnivorous, and poisons its prey with a sting.

Mitre family
About 3 cm long
Province: Lusitanian
Named by Lamarck in 1811

Little Trumpet Mitre

This snail is similar to the Ebony Mitre, but slightly smaller. There are no ribs on its shell, and no teeth on the outer edge of the aperture. The shell is glossy brown in colour. It is a common species of the Mediterranean, and is also found along the coast of Portugal and the Azores.

Mitre family
About 2 cm long
Province: Lusitanian
Named by Linnaeus in 1758

Mediterranean Cone

Most cone shells live in warm waters; this specimen is the only one found as far north as Portugal. It is common in the Mediterranean. It has an elongated cone-shaped shell with a short, flattish spire and a long aperture. The colour varies, but most specimens are a dull brown. The snail has hollow, harpoon-shaped teeth on its radula (tongue), with which it injects poison into its prey.

Cone family
About 2.5 cm long
Province: Lusitanian
Named by Gmelin in 1791

Striate Pisania

Also called the Grooved Pisania, this little whelk lives on rocks between the high and low tide lines and also on rocks in shallow water. it is a carnivore. It is common in the Mediterranean and as far south as the Azores. Note the strongly-toothed aperture.

Whelk family
About 3 cm long
Province: Lusitanian
Named by
Gmelin in 1791

Milky Ark

This tiny bivalve lives attached to rocks in sandy areas, and is common from the southern coast of Britain to the Mediterranean. Its shell is thick, coloured yellowish-white with a light-brown over-layer. The hinge plate has forty to fifty small teeth.

Ark family
About 1 cm long
Provinces: Celtic, Lusitanian
Named by Linnaeus in 1767

European Cerith

This snail has a long shell with a pointed spire. Its shell is heavily sculptured with rows of knobs. The colour varies from whitish to grey or brown. It lives in shallow water off-shore, feeding on vegetable matter. It is very common in the Mediterranean, and less common on nearby Atlantic coasts.

Horn Shell family
About 7.5 cm long
Province: Lusitanian
Named by Brugière in 1792

Noah's Ark

Ark shells have long, sturdy shells. In the Noah's Ark the shell varies in shape. There is a straight hinge with small interlocking teeth. The outside is dark-brown in colour, flecked with lighter markings, and with a brown over-layer. It attaches itself to rocks by strong threads just below the low tide line, in the Mediterranean and on Atlantic coasts.

Ark family
About 6 cm long
Province: Lusitanian
Named by Linnaeus in 1758

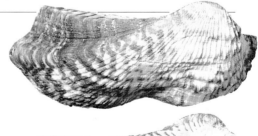

Blue Mussel

The Blue Mussel is also known as the Edible Mussel or Common Mussel. The outside of its shell is a deep blue-black in colour. The inner shell is nearly white with a deep-blue border. This bivalve lives in large colonies attached to rocks from near high-water mark downward. At low tide it shuts its valves firmly to keep the moisture in. It is edible, but be sure to take mussels only from unpolluted areas. You may find it from northern Europe through the Mediterranean to the Black Sea.

Mussel family
About 6.5 cm or more
Provinces: Boreal,
Celtic, Lusitanian
Named by
Linnaeus in 1758

Mediterranean Blue Mussel

This bivalve is similar to the Blue Mussel, but is usually larger, broader, and more curved. The mantle edge of the animal is blue-black, while that of the Blue Mussel is straw-coloured. It is a common species in Western Europe, and is often farmed.

Mussel family
About 10 cm long
Province: Lusitanian
Named by Lamarck in 1822

Northern Horse Mussel

The adult shell is chalky white with a shiny brown skin. It is strong and oblong, and the beak or umbo is not right at the tip. It has no hinge teeth. The mature animal is orange-brown. It is common in northern waters, as far south as the British Isles and France, and can form huge colonies with many thousands of individuals.

Mussel family
About 10 cm long
Provinces: Boreal, Celtic

Bearded Horse Mussel

The Bearded Horse Mussel is small. Its shell is broad at one end, coloured yellow and reddish. It is covered with a thick, yellow-brown, hairy over-layer. This bivalve lives under rocks and on seaweeds from the low tide line seawards. It is common from the southern British Isles into the Mediterranean.

Mussel family
About 7 cm long
Provinces:
Celtic, Lusitanian
Named by
Linnaeus in 1758

Discord Mussel

You will find this mussel on the lower half of the shore, attached to seaweeds. It also flourishes off-shore. It is common from the British Isles to the Mediterranean. Its shell is shaped like a kidney bean and is fairly fragile. It is smooth and reddish in colour, with a brown to black over-layer. The interior is bluish-white.

Mussel family
About 4 cm long
Provinces: Celtic, Lusitanian
Named by Linnaeus in 1767

Adriatic Horse Mussel

The shell of this bivalve is brittle and bulbous, with the beaks close to, but not at the front end. The outside is yellow with reddish rays or irregular zigzag streaks. The inside is nearly white, with the external rays showing through. This is an off-shore species, found from the British Isles south to the Mediterranean.

Mussel family
About 4 cm long
Provinces: Celtic, Lusitanian
Named by Lamarck in 1822

Saddle Jingle Shell

Also known as the Saddle Oyster, this bivalve is common from the middle shoreline seawards. Its range is from Scandinavia to the Mediterranean. The lower valve is smaller, flatter, and more fragile than the upper valve. The shell is white in colour, with occasional mottling of pink or purple. Its shell usually takes on the shape of the shell or other object to which the Jingle Shell is attached.

Jingle Shell family
About 5 cm long
Provinces: Boreal,
Celtic, Lusitanian
Named by
Linnaeus in 1758

Explore the Shore

The shells you find depend on what kind of beach you explore. The best beaches to search are sandy and muddy ones for burrowing molluscs, and rocky ones for the molluscs that hide in crevices, cling to rocks, or are stranded in rock pools.

You will not find many shells on a shingle (pebble) beach, because the sea moves the stones about, smashing empty shells and making life impossible for living molluscs. At low tide the shingle dries out, which again is not a good habitat for sea-snails and bivalves.

Beach zones

You can divide every beach into five zones (shown below). They are governed by the rise and fall of the tide. High tide occurs every twelve hours and twenty-five minutes, and low tide is about six hours and thirteen minutes after high tide. You can find out from tide tables when the next low tide is due.

Roughly twice a month, the tides produce very high water and very low water. These are called **spring** tides, although they are nothing to do with the season of spring. In between these are the **neap** tides, which do not come up so high or go down so low as spring tides. The shore between the highest point covered by the tides and the lowest point uncovered by them is the **intertidal** zone, and that is where you will do most of your exploring.

Make a beach map

If you are on the beach around low tide, why not make a map of the tidal zones? All you need is a long piece of string, a tape measure, a notebook, and a pencil.

1 **Tie one end of the string** to a rock or piece of driftwood and put it just above the line of rubbish that marks the edge of the splash zone.
2 **Tie the other end** to a rock or stick and place it at the edge of the water.

The SPLASH ZONE is wetted by spray at high tide, but is only covered when storms drive waves on to the beach.

The UPPER ZONE is often uncovered even at high tide.

The MIDDLE ZONE is the largest area. It is always uncovered at low tide.

The LOWER ZONE is uncovered by spring tides.

The SHALLOW WATER ZONE is always covered by water even at low tide.

Cockle Bay - 3rd June   LOW TIDE

3 metre Splash Zone	Periwinkles / Brown Seaweed
7 metre Upper Zone	Razorshell / Green Seaweed
15 metre Middle Zone	oil / old rope / crab claw
10 metre Lower Zone	mussels / cockle

3 **Use pebbles or driftwood** to show where the different zones start.

4 **Measure each zone with the tape** and record how far it stretches.

5 **Make a list of what you find in each zone** – shells, sea weed, pollution items (see right), and anything else of interest. Is there a band of pebbles or an outcrop of rocks?

6 **When you go to another beach** and do this survey again, compare the two maps to see how the beaches differ.

Pollution survey

It is a good exercise, best done by a group of you, to patrol a beach and make a list of what is on it that shouldn't be. Try to work out for yourself where the various kinds of pollution have come from. These are some of the things to look out for:

1 **Glass**: mostly bottles and often broken.

2 **Plastic and polythene**: plastic sometimes breaks up, but polythene bottles and bags don't.

3 **Wood**: some is washed down by rivers; the rest is from boats or old shore structures.

4 **Canisters and barrels**: these often still have their contents, which can range from chemicals to food. They don't always have a label to tell you what is inside. **Don't touch these**, but report them to the nearest coastguard, the police, or the local authority as soon as possible. **They may be dangerous.**

5 **Oil**: usually as patches of black tar, which can be very difficult to remove from your clothes. Use olive oil on a pad of cotton to clean up.

6 **Dead fish and sea birds**: these are usually victims of oil spillages.

7 **Wire, plain or barbed.**

8 **Bits of metal**, such as sheets of corrugated iron.

9 **Sewage**: this covers anything that goes down your toilet, plus disposable nappies.

Pollution of our beaches is a major problem these days. Some is rubbish discarded by thoughtless people using the beaches, but a lot of rubbish comes from ships and is washed ashore. In some areas pollution is caused by sewage which has been pumped out to sea, but has then been washed back to the shore by the tide.

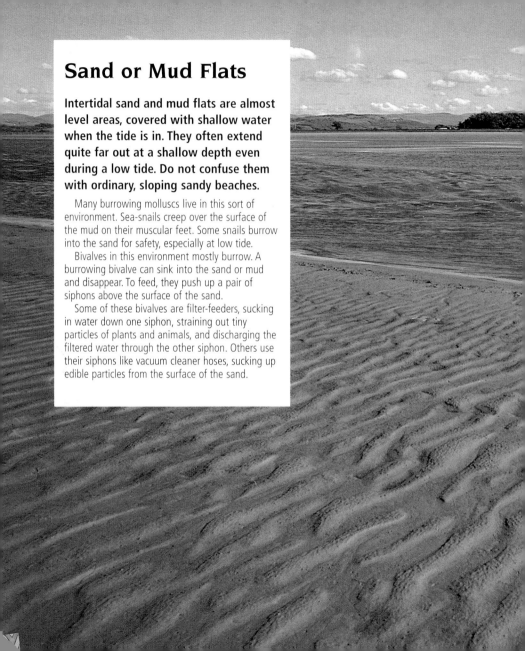

Sand or Mud Flats

Intertidal sand and mud flats are almost level areas, covered with shallow water when the tide is in. They often extend quite far out at a shallow depth even during a low tide. Do not confuse them with ordinary, sloping sandy beaches.

Many burrowing molluscs live in this sort of environment. Sea-snails creep over the surface of the mud on their muscular feet. Some snails burrow into the sand for safety, especially at low tide.

Bivalves in this environment mostly burrow. A burrowing bivalve can sink into the sand or mud and disappear. To feed, they push up a pair of siphons above the surface of the sand.

Some of these bivalves are filter-feeders, sucking in water down one siphon, straining out tiny particles of plants and animals, and discharging the filtered water through the other siphon. Others use their siphons like vacuum cleaner hoses, sucking up edible particles from the surface of the sand.

Exasperating Topshell

These little shells come in a variety of patterns of reds, browns and tans. They are small, solid and pyramid-shaped, with a high spire and flat sides. They are sculptured with three or four large, rounded, beaded cords. They live on eel grasses, which flourish in this habitat. The species is fairly common from southern England south into the Mediterranean.

Topshell family
About 1 cm long
Provinces: Celtic, Lusitanian
Named by Pennant in 1777

Baby Pheasant Shell

Pheasant shells are so named because of their many colours. Most of them are tiny, like these Baby Pheasant Shells. The shell is solid and semi-translucent, and is taller than it is broad. There are many colour variations, involving shades of red and yellow, with red and brown markings. It is a fairly common shallow-water species, ranging from the southern British Isles to the Adriatic Sea and the Azores.

Pheasant Shell family
About 1 cm long
Provinces: Celtic, Lusitanian
Named by Linnaeus in 1758

Beautiful Pheasant Shell

This slightly larger pheasant shell is a locally-common shallow-water species ranging from Portugal to the Mediterranean. The shell is elongated, thin and glossy. It is coloured with red and white flames, spiral rows of red dots and oblique lines of pink or yellow.

Pheasant Shell family
About 2 cm long
Province: Lusitanian
Named by Mühlfeld in 1824

Striate Cingula

This snail and the next two belong to a group of extremely small animals known as rissoid snails. There are hundreds of species, which are difficult to tell apart. The Striate Cingula has a tall-spired, elongated shell, varying from white to rusty brown. It is very common in shallow water, usually among weeds and stones, from southern Norway to the British Isles and the Mediterranean.

Rissoid Snail family – About 1.5–3 mm
Provinces: Boreal, Celtic, Lusitanian
Named by Montagu in 1803

Parchment Rissoa

This rissoid snail has a long, turreted shell, usually with about a dozen axial ribs per whorl. It is white or yellowish-parchment in colour. The shape is variable. Snails from brackish water have smooth, slender, semi-transparent shells. Those from ocean water are fatter with heavier ribbing. The range is from Norway and the Baltic Sea to the Canary Islands.

Rissoid Snail family
About 7 mm long – Provinces: Boreal, Celtic, Lusitanian
Named by J. Adams in 1800

Bug Alvania

The Bug Alvania is a rissoid snail with a squat, oval shell, covered with spiral rows of tiny beads. It is whitish with brown bands. It is common locally in shallow water from France south into the Mediterranean.

Rissoid Snail family
About 3–5 mm
Provinces: Celtic, Lusitanian
Named by Linnaeus in 1758

Lurid Cowrie

Like all cowries, this shell is very glossy. It is a lightweight, egg-shaped shell, white underneath and inside, and fawnish-brown on top with darker streaks. It is common in shallow water. Its range is from the Mediterranean south down the African coast.

Cowrie family
About 4.5 cm long
Province: Lusitanian
Named by Linnaeus in 1758

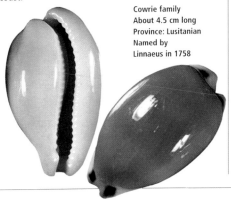

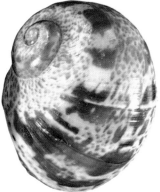

Dusky Moon Snail

This is a southern Mediterranean species which extends northward to the British Isles wherever there is shallow water and a sandy, muddy bottom. It has a brown or chestnut shell, which is globe-shaped with a small rounded spire. When fresh, the shell is covered with a dull, dark over-layer. The lower aperture is white and the trapdoor operculum is brown or sometimes chalky.

Moon Snail family
About 3 cm long
Provinces: Celtic, Lusitanian
Named by Blainville in 1825

Hebrew Moon Snail

This snail is more colourful than many other species of necklace or moon shells. It has a variegated pattern of brown and white. The trapdoor operculum is white. It is moderately common off-shore on sand and gravel. Its range is western Europe and the Mediterranean.

Moon Snail family
About 5 cm long
Provinces: Celtic, Lusitanian
Named by von Salis in 1793

European Necklace Shell

The globe-shaped shell is tan-coloured, with smooth, well-rounded whorls. The trapdoor operculum is brown. It catches its bivalve prey by holding it with its foot, and drilling a hole in the shell with acid from its radula (tongue). The snail is common on intertidal sand flats, ranging from the British Isles to the Mediterranean.

Moon Snail family
About 4 cm long
Provinces: Celtic, Lusitanian
Named by da Costa in 1778

Watery Paper-bubble

Bubble Shell family
About 1 cm long
Provinces: Celtic, Lusitanian
Named by Linnaeus in 1758

A snail that feeds on small bivalves, the Watery Paper-bubble has a fragile, globe-shaped shell, with a very large aperture. In colour it is a translucent white or pale yellow. The animal is light-brown, and the mantle covers most of the shell. The snail is found in muddy sand in subtidal areas from the British Isles to the Mediterranean.

Bubble Akera

The akera snail carries its fragile shell on its hind end. The animal is elongated. It has side flaps to its mantle, which it uses for swimming at spawning time in the spring, and wraps over the shell at other times. The animal is pale grey to orange, with many small black and white spots and streaks. If disturbed it may emit a purple fluid. It may be found on mud flats at low tide, from Norway through the British Isles to the Mediterranean.

Bubble Shell family
About 2 cm long
Provinces: Boreal, Celtic, Lusitanian
Named by Müller in 1776

Common Turret Shell

Another name for this snail is the Tower Shell. The shell is very long and thin, with about fifteen spirally-ridged whorls. It is brownish-yellow, with the base tinged with lilac. It lives in sand just off the shore, but empty shells are cast up on the beach. It is very common in muddy, shallow waters from Norway to North Africa.

Turret Shell family
About 2.5–6 cm long
Provinces: Boreal, Celtic, Lusitanian
Named by Risso in 1829

Thickened Nassa

Another name for this snail is the Thick-lipped Dog Whelk. It has a small, thick shell with a sharp spire and a small aperture surrounded by a thickened lip. There are five whorls with ten to twelve rounded axial ribs. The colour is reddish-buff to yellow-grey. It is common in large colonies in muddy areas, in most of western Europe and the Mediterranean.

Nassa Mud Snail family
About 1 cm long
Provinces: Celtic, Lusitanian
Named by Ström in 1768

Netted Dog Whelk

Reticulated Nassa is another name for this snail. Both names come about because it looks as though it is wearing a hair-net. It has a solid, heavy, coarse shell, which is sculptured with beads, knobs and ribs. The colour is glossy white, with fine brown spiral lines and occasional dark blotches. These scavengers live in pockets of soft sand among rocky intertidal areas, and range from the Black Sea northward to the British Isles and Norway.

Nassa Mud Snail family
Up to 3 cm long – Provinces: Boreal, Celtic, Lusitanian
Named by Linnaeus in 1758

Little Horn Nassa

The shell of this little mud snail is elongated, and the aperture extends for about half its length. The colour is a rosy tan, with small cream flames, and small dots on the broad, light-brown spiral bands. It is common on muddy flats in the Mediterranean and the Iberian Peninsula.

Nassa Mud Snail family
About 1 cm long
Provinces: Celtic, Lusitanian
Named by Olivi in 1792

Donax Tellin

This bivalve has a small, thin shell, with the right valve slightly more convex than the left valve. The colour varies from grey to yellowish, with pink rays, while some shells are all white. There are many evenly spaced concentric ridges. It is a common shallow-water species, living in coarse sand from Orkney south to the Black Sea and the Azores.

Tellin family
About 2.5 cm long
Provinces: Boreal, Celtic, Lusitanian
Named by Linnaeus in 1758

Fleshy Tellin

The shell is an elongated oval, coloured pink, with a narrow, white radial ray at the pointed rear end. It flourishes in sand in shallow water, mainly in the Mediterranean. It is sometimes found further north, as far as northern Portugal.

Tellin family
About 2.5 cm long
Province: Lusitanian
Named by Linnaeus in 1758

Flat Tellin

A fairly large, compressed shell distinguishes this bivalve. The outside of the shell is white, smoothish, with weak concentric scratches. The over-layer is thin and brownish. It is found on sand bars in the Mediterranean, and from Portugal south to West Africa.

Tellin family
About 6.5 cm long
Province: Lusitanian
Named by Linnaeus in 1758

Violet Bittersweet

A burrowing bivalve, it usually lives in sandy or muddy gravel. The solid shell is almost circular in outline, with numerous clearly defined ribs. The hinge has many, small, equal-sized teeth. It is a Mediterranean species. A slightly larger (7 cm), related species, known as the Dog Cockle, lives in the Celtic province, including in British waters.

Dog Cockle family
About 6 cm long – Province: Lusitania
Named by Lamarck in 1819

Sand Cockle

This Mediterranean species has a broadly oval shell, with about thirty-five small radial ribs. The ribs at the front end have smooth rounded scales, and those at the rear have short spines. The colour is yellow-brown. The bivalve ranges north to Portugal.

Cockle family
About 6.5 cm
Province: Lusitanian
Named by Lightfoot in 1786

Hians Cockle

The strong shell of this bivalve has bold radial ribs, with spines on them. There is a wide gape at the rear end. It is a fairly common southerly species, living from the low tide line to thirty metres deep. Its range is from the Atlantic coast of Spain to the Mediterranean.

Cockle family
About 7.5 cm long
Provinces: Celtic, Lusitanian
Named by Brocchi in 1814

Tuberculate Cockle

A bivalve common in shallow water from the British Isles to the Mediterranean, the Tuberculate Cockle has an elongated oval shell. It bears twenty-one to twenty-three prominent radial ribs, with small tubercles or beads on them. The colour is light brown. The animal lives off-shore in sand.

Cockle family
About 6.5 cm – Provinces: Celtic, Lusitanian
Named by Linnaeus in 1758

Warty Venus Shell

The Warty Venus Shell is almost circular in outline. It has strong concentric ridges, broken up near the edge into heart-shaped 'warts'. It is brownish-cream to greyish-white in colour. It is a common edible clam, ranging from the British Isles to the Mediterranean, the Canary Islands and South Africa.

Venus Clam family
About 6.5 cm long
Provinces:
Celtic, Lusitanian
Named by
Linnaeus in 1758

Crosscut Carpet Shell

Decussate Venus is another name for this sand-burrowing bivalve, whose shells are often washed up on the beach. It is roughly oval in shape, with many small radial ribs crossed by fine concentric growth lines – hence its popular name. It has colours of greys, yellows and browns, sometimes with rays and streaks. It is common in shallow water from Norway to the Mediterranean.

Venus Clam family – About 5 cm long
Provinces: Boreal, Celtic, Lusitanian
Named by Linnaeus in 1758

Rayed Trough Shell

Also called the Rayed Trough Clam, this bivalve is widely distributed from Norway to the Black Sea, and south to Senegal. It burrows into clean sand just off-shore. It has a brittle oval shell, creamy white with purple around the beaks, and usually with brown rays. The over-layer is light brown. Empty shells are often washed up.

Trough Clam family
About 4 cm long
Provinces: Boreal,
Celtic, Lusitanian
Named by
Linnaeus in 1758

Sand or Mud Flats

Four-sided Ark

The box-shaped shell gives this ark clam its popular
name. It is a sturdy shell, with widely separated
beaks in the front half. The gape in the shell allows
the massive green byssus thread space to attach
itself to a rock. The outside of the shell is yellowish
to dirty white, with a brown over-layer. It is
common in shallow water from Norway to the
Mediterranean.

Ark Clam family
About 3 cm long – Provinces: Boreal, Celtic, Lusitanian
Named by Poli in 1795

Truncate Wedge-clam

A southern species, the Truncate Wedge-clam is
similar to the Banded Wedge-shell, but the front
end of its valve is shorter and more rounded. It is
tan coloured, with purplish rays. There is a tan,
glossy, translucent over-layer. It can be found on
sand flats from Portugal to the Black Sea.

Wedge Clam family
About 3 cm long
Province: Celtic,
Lusitanian
Named by
Linnaeus
in 1758

Tellin-like Sunset Clam

Sunset clams are similar in appearance to tellins,
but are usually larger. This species is small. It has a
solid, elongated oval shell, creamy-white with tints
of orange, red or purple. The shell is sculptured
with wide concentric and radiating lines. It is a
common shallow-water clam, fond from Iceland
and Norway to the Mediterranean.

Sunset Clam family
About 2.5 cm long – Provinces: Boreal, Celtic, Lusitanian
Named by Lamarck in 1818

White Abra Clam

This small clam is common in muddy gravel, from
the low tide line downward. It is also found in
estuaries and creeks. It has a brittle, white shell,
usually glossy. Its valves have a weak, narrow hinge.
It ranges from Norway to the Black Sea and as far
south as Senegal.

Furrow Clam family
About 2 cm long
Provinces:
Boreal, Celtic, Lusitanian
Named by
Wood in 1815

Flat Furrow Clam

The intertidal region is home for the Flat Furrow Clam. Its shell is more or less round in outline, fairly compressed. The beaks are almost at the centre of the valves. The colour is greyish-brown or light yellow. Its range is from Norway to as far south as Senegal.

Furrow Clam family – About 6.5 cm long
Provinces: Boreal, Celtic, Lusitanian
Named by da Costa in 1778

Common Basket Shell

The flatter and smaller left valve fits into the right valve like a lid in a basket – hence the popular name. The shell is cream with a brown over-layer. It is very common in shallow water over sand or mud. Its range is from Norway to the Mediterranean and West Africa.

Furrow Clam family
About 1 cm long
Provinces: Boreal, Celtic, Lusitanian
Named by Olivi in 1792

Sand Gaper

Gapers get their name from the large gape at the rear end where the siphons stick out. They are also called soft-shell clams, because their chalky shells are easily broken. The Sand Gaper has a white to greyish shell, with a thin over-layer of grey or straw colour. It is very common in the intertidal zone of sand and mud flats. Its European range is from Norway to France. On the Atlantic coast of North America it is a popular food.

Soft-shell Clam family
About 10 cm long
Provinces: Boreal, Celtic
Named by Linnaeus in 1758

Sand or Mud Flats

Giant Razor Clam

Another name for this bivalve is the Pod Razor. It is the largest European razor shell. The valves are almost straight, with rounded, gaping ends. They are white, with reddish streaks and blotches. The over-layer is dark green. It is common at low tide line, and is much sought by collectors. It is found from Norway south to the Mediterranean.

Razor Clam family
About 20 cm long
Provinces: Boreal,
Celtic, Lusitanian
Named by
Linnaeus in 1758

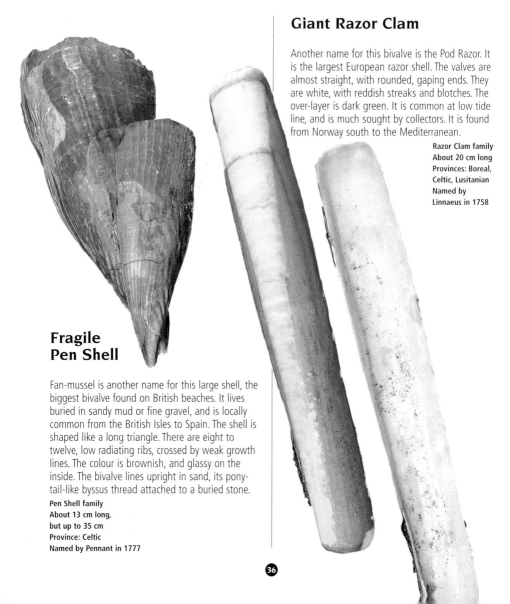

Fragile Pen Shell

Fan-mussel is another name for this large shell, the biggest bivalve found on British beaches. It lives buried in sandy mud or fine gravel, and is locally common from the British Isles to Spain. The shell is shaped like a long triangle. There are eight to twelve, low radiating ribs, crossed by weak growth lines. The colour is brownish, and glassy on the inside. The bivalve lines upright in sand, its pony-tail-like byssus thread attached to a buried stone.

Pen Shell family
About 13 cm long,
but up to 35 cm
Province: Celtic
Named by Pennant in 1777

Narrow Jackknife Clam

This is one of the smaller razor shells. It is fairly common in silty sand. Its slightly curved valves taper at the rear end, and are rounded at the front or burrowing end. The shell is tan and white, with reddish-brown blotches and a greenish over-layer. It ranges from Norway to the Mediterranean

Razor Clam family
About 10 cm long – Provinces: Boreal, Celtic, Lusitanian
Named by Linnaeus in 1758

Strigate Razor Clam

This burrowing clam is a close relative of the Bean Razor Clam. Its name comes from a Latin word for a scraper used by Roman bathers. In shape the shell is oblong, with gaping, rounded ends. The outside is pinkish, with a yellowish-green over-layer. It is found in the Mediterranean, and on the Atlantic coast of France.

Tagelus Razor Clam family – About 5 cm long
Provinces: Celtic, Lusitanian
Named by Linnaeus in 1758

Bean Razor Clam

Another name for this clam is the Pod Shell. It looks like a true razor shell, but is actually a distant relative of the tellins. You can tell the difference because its hinge is almost in the middle of the valves, while in true razor shells the hinge is near one end. The Bean Razor Clam has a long, cylindrical shell, yellowish-white with a yellowish-green over-layer. It is common from Norway to the Mediterranean.

Tagelus Razor Clam family
About 13 cm long
Provinces: Boreal, Celtic, Lusitanian
Named by Linnaeus in 1758

Collecting Expedition

To make your expedition a success you need the right clothing and equipment. It doesn't really matter what you wear as long as it suits the weather. Remember that the sun at the beach can be very strong, and you can easily be burned. So you should use a sun-screen cream, and may need to wear a thin T-shirt and sun-hat. Read the Collector's Code (page 2) before you start.

However, it is important what you put on your feet. On soft sand and mud it's fun to go barefoot, but a lot of litter is washed on to beaches these days, and it can include sharp objects such as cans, broken glass, and jagged pieces of plastic. On rocky beaches the rocks themselves can cause cuts, so always have boots or shoes with you.

Where to look

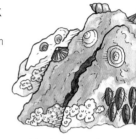

On a rocky shore you can find live limpets and periwinkles clinging to rocks. You will also find barnacles and mussels there, and the sea-snails that prey on them, such as whelks.

Some periwinkles hide in cracks in the rocks. If a mollusc has burrowed into the rock by drilling a hole, it is probably a piddock (see pages 74–77). Other piddocks, and the destructive shipworms, bore into wood. Examine pieces of driftwood to see if you can find them.

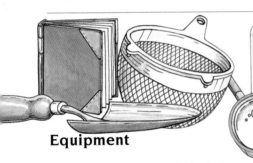

Equipment

The following equipment is useful for finding specimens, examining and recording them, and taking them home.

1 **A spade or trowel** is essential on sand and mud to dig up live borrowing molluscs.
2 **A fine kitchen sieve** to strain out very small shells.
3 **A clear-plastic box** to inspect pools with on windy days.
4 **A good magnifying glass** to examine specimens closely. Buy one of the small folding type with a magnification of x 10.
5 **A field notebook** to keep a record of what you find and where (see opposite).
6 **A waterproof pen.**
7 **A plastic bucket**, with a lid is best, for transporting live specimens. Fill it with seawater.
8 **Small plastic bags** for empty shells.
9 **A light backpack** to carry everything in.

Breakwaters, posts, and piers on sand beaches are also worth checking.

If you pick up a live mollusc to examine it you should put it back afterward where you found it. If you want to take it home, turn to pages 44–45 which explain how to care for live molluscs.

Live bivalves are generally hiding in burrows in sand or mud. This is where you will need your spade to dig them out. It is not an easy task, and razor shells in particular are more skilled at hiding than you will be at finding them. You are just as likely to uncover marine worms. It will pay you to sieve the sand or mud as you dig, because so many molluscs are tiny.

Be prepared to turn over rocks or peer under them. Some sea-snails live on seaweeds, and are probably on the under side, but always roll them back after you have looked.

Use the clear-plastic box to look in rock pools on windy days without disturbing the occupants. You can often find a rich haul of molluscs which have been exposed as the tide goes out. Check under the overhang of the rocks, and lift up seaweeds.

Keeping a record

Your field notebook is essential for recording how and where you found shells, and any interesting information about the beach and the nearby area.

1 **When you go to a new beach**, give it a special number and make a note of the date and what sort of habitats it has (rock pools, sand flats, etc). Why not take a photo for your record file (right)?
2 **Each time you visit** that beach, record where the tide was and what the weather was like.
3 **When you find a mollusc or an empty shell**, make a note of the habitat in which you found it, whether any other molluscs were around, and what other creatures or features were nearby.
4 **Write the beach's special number** on the outside of each bag, add the date, and number the bag as well. Use the same bag number in your notebook, so that you can match up your notes to the bags.

Cockle Bay
Rocky pools

3-7-93

Estuaries & Lagoons

The waters of river estuaries contain a mixture of salt water from the sea and fresh water. As a result the water is brackish (or slightly salty). The amount of salt depends on how much fresh water is flowing down the river. Only certain species of molluscs do well in this semi-salt water.

Brackish water also occurs in lagoons. These are shallow bodies of water close to the sea. They are usually found in enclosed seas, such as the Baltic and the Mediterranean, where the rise and fall of the tides is small. They are also to be found along coasts where there are sand dunes – for example in the south-west of France.

Lagoons are separated from the sea by narrow strips of sand or pebbles, called barrier islands. A British example of a barrier island is the Chesil Bank in Dorset, which shelters the East and West Fleet channels.

Pointed Cingula

The Pointed Cingula belongs to a family of extremely small snails — so tiny that a ladle will hold dozens of them. There are hundreds of different species. The Pointed Cingula is shown here as an example of how small these snails can be. It lives among seaweed in shallow, brackish water, from Scandinavia to the northern British Isles.

Rissoid Snail family
About 3 mm long – Province: Boreal
Named by Gould in 1841

Atlantic Oyster Drill

This little snail is the biggest enemy of oysters. It drills a hole in the oyster shell and sucks out the soft body. It destroys well over half the crop in some commercial oyster beds. Its colour is a dirty grey or yellow, with a brown aperture. It is a North American species that was accidentally introduced to England about 1920, and is slowly spreading.

Murex and Rock Shell family
About 4 cm long – Province: Celtic
Named by T. Say in 1822

Mouse Melampus

This is a typical marsh snail, generally found in estuaries. It has a tiny, barrel-shaped shell, dark-brown and semi-glossy. It breathes air. The animal is a hermaphrodite, combining both sexes. It is locally common in marshes on estuaries in north-western Europe.

Marsh Snail family
About 7 mm long – Province: Celtic
Named by Draparnaud in 1801

Common Oyster

The Edible Oyster, as it is called, is also known as the 'Native' Oyster because it was for many years the only common European species. It has an almost circular shell, rough with deep ribs. The upper valve is flat and brownish. It is common off-shore from Norway to the Black Sea, and is cultivated in oyster beds.

Oyster family
About 10 cm long
Provinces: Boreal, Celtic, Lusitanian
Named by Linnaeus in 1758

Portuguese Oyster

This is the Giant Pacific Oyster, which was introduced to Europe (with a change of name) many years ago. It is twice the size of the Common Oyster, with a long shell of varying shape. There are several coarse ridges. It is found on the sand and gravel off coasts in the North Sea, English Channel, the Atlantic Ocean and the Mediterranean.

Oyster family
Up to 30 cm long
Provinces: Celtic, Lusitania
Named by Thunberg in 1793

European Thorny Oyster

Thorny oysters are popular with collectors because of their sculpture. The shell is thick, reddish-brown or violet on the outside, and a glossy white inside. Radiating ribs on the upper valve carry a series of long, sharp spines. The hinge bears two 'ball-and-socket' teeth. It is found on rocks in shallow water, in the Mediterranean and further north than Portugal.

Thorny Oyster family
About 7.5 cm long – Province: Lusitanian
Named by Linnaeus in 1758

Edible Cockle

The Edible or Common European Cockle is a favourite food for seaside visitors in England. The larvae settle in huge beds of up to 10,000 animals per square metre, in estuaries from Norway to Portugal and West Africa. In some places the cockles are farmed commercially. The off-white or brown shell is solid, almost oval, with rolled-in beaks almost touching each other. There are twenty-two to twenty-eight squarish radial ribs.

Cockle family – About 4 cm long
Provinces: Boreal, Celtic, Lusitanian
Named by Linnaeus in 1758

Zebra Mussel

This little bivalve belongs to a family known as the False Mussels. They thrive in salt, brackish or fresh water. The Zebra Mussel originated in the Baltic Sea, and retains many characteristics of sea mussels. It is common in some British lakes and rivers. It gets its name from the zebra-like stripes on its tan-coloured shell.

False Mussel family
About 2.5 cm long
Provinces: Boreal, Celtic
Named by Pallas in 1771

Baltic Tellin

This bivalve is also called the Baltic Macoma, and is very common in the Baltic Sea, where it can tolerate the low saltiness of the water. It is found in shallow water on muddy bottoms. The shell is small and oval. The colour varies, but is often whitish or tinged with pink or purple. The over-layer is thin and grey, and it flakes off when the shell is dry. Its range is from the Arctic south to Portugal.

Tellin family
About 2.5 cm long
Provinces:
Celtic, Lusitanian
Named by
Linnaeus in 1758

Studying Live Molluscs

If you take live specimens home to study, you must have a suitable place to keep them. Never keep them away from their natural habitat for more than a week and only study a few at a time.

The shorter the time you keep them the better. One reason for this is that it is difficult to arrange a suitable supply of food for a mollusc unless you know exactly what it eats. If in doubt always ask somebody who knows, such as a biology teacher or a more experienced collector.

You can observe sea-snails in large glass jars, and you may find it as well to keep predatory animals, such as whelks, on their own in this way. You can feed them bits of meat. Thawed frozen shrimps are also enjoyed by carnivores. **Don't feed them more than once or twice a week** and remove the food that is not eaten that evening.

A seawater aquarium

The best place to keep specimens is in a regular aquarium. You can buy one in a shop that specializes in fish tanks. Such a tank should be large enough to allow for a good layer of sand or gravel on the bottom – a 20 or 40 litre tank is large enough.

Concentrate on specimens of species that require a similar environment. When you want to study something that needs a different habitat you should clean out the tank and start again.

The dealer who sells you the tank should advise you on what else you need. The equipment may include a filter, but this may remove the small algae that bivalves eat; and an air pump, to make sure the water has enough oxygen in it. (Sea animals absorb oxygen from the water, just as you do from the air you breathe.)

Because you are studying sea-water specimens, you will need to have enough sea-water to fill the tank. Ask an adult to take a supply home for you by car, in a watertight container.

Mark the water level on the side of the aquarium and when it goes down, you can top it up with rain or pond water. Put a sheet of glass or plastic over the tank to stop the water evaporating, but leave a crack for air to circulate.

Decorating your aquarium

Try to create a realistic environment for your molluscs. Rocks with algae on them, from the seaside, will appeal to many sea snails, such as periwinkles, and provide food. Some seaweed will help the appearance of the tank, and also help to provide a balanced environment.

Aquariums always function best with a layer of clean pea-gravel in the bottom. But if you want to study a mollusc that lives in mud or sand you will have to add a solid layer of sand in at least part of the tank, for them to burrow into. This should be 2.5–5 centimetres deep.

The water in a sea-water aquarium should be as near as possible the same temperature as the sea. Bear this in mind when deciding where to put your aquarium. For example, it wouldn't be a good idea to put it on a window sill in direct sunlight. On the other hand, remember that in winter the sea, even near the shore, can be warmer than freshwater ponds or rivers.

Things you might see

The eye of a gastropod peeping out of its shell (this is a Pink Conch)

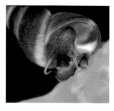

The Common Northern Chink Shell on the move with its foot extended

A Cockle with its siphons showing. This means that it is drawing in water to gather oxygen so that it can breathe

A pair of Slipper-shells mating – see they are connected at the top right

Egg clusters of the Common Northern Chink Shell

Intertidal Rocks & Sand

Much of the European coast is made up of a mixture of rocks and sand. Unless the shore is pounded constantly and violently by the waves, the first thing you will probably notice about these shorelines is the rich mass of seaweeds exposed when the tide is out.

These seaweeds are generally green or brown, though some of the so-called red seaweeds are more brownish in colour. The seaweed provides food for many species of molluscs, and shelter for even more. The seaweeds keep the heat of the sun off, and also help to prevent them from drying out at low tide.

You are unlikely to find many of the off-shore species of molluscs alive, but their shells are frequently washed up on the beach. Species you are likely to encounter include slit limpets, topshells, wentletraps and moon snails. If you are lucky you may occasionally find live species at very low water during spring tides.

Intertidal Rocks & Sand

European Painted Topshell

Topshells are cone-shaped, with almost flat bases. The straight sides of this shell make it look like a miniature bell-tent. It occurs in many different colours, including a rare, pure white form. It is moderately common among small stones and weeds from the low tide line downward, and may be found in rock pools. The animals has four extra pairs of tentacles on its body. The range is from Norway to the Mediterranean.

Topshell family – About 2.5 cm long
Provinces: Boreal, Celtic, Lusitanian
Named by Linnaeus in 1758

Horn Topshell

The Horn Topshell has a narrower, higher shell than the Painted Topshell. It is flesh-coloured with alternating blotches of white and brown. The surface is highly polished. The snail is a shallow-water species, fairly common in the Mediterranean, and extending to Portugal, the Azores and the Canary Islands.

Topshell family
About 2.5 cm long
Province: Lusitanian
Named by Linnaeus in 1758

Rough Star-shell

Another name for this shell is the Rugose Turban. It is one of the few turban shells that does not live in tropical waters. The shell is about as high as it is wide. It is solid and heavy, and the whorls carry three rows of short spines. The colour is often reddish-brown. It is common in shallow water, from Portugal into the Mediterranean and the Azores.

Turban Shell family
About 5 cm long
Province: Lusitanian
Named by Dillwyn in 1758

Heavy Slit Limpet

Slit limpets are not true limpets, but emarginulas. They are very like true limpets, except that they have a small slit in the front edge of the shell for getting rid of water and waste products. This slit limpet, also called the Crass Emarginula, is one of several that live on subtidal rocks. The small white shells are coiled in their young stages, but grow into shield-shapes. The range of this species is from Iceland and Norway to Scotland and Ireland.

Keyhole Limpet family
About 2.5 cm long
Province: Boreal
Named by Sowerby in 1813

Common Northern Chink Shell

A tiny chink on one side of the aperture gives this periwinkle its common name. It is also called the Common Northern Lacuna. The tiny shell is thin but strong, and translucent. It is light tan in colour, with a hint of purplish-rose on the spire. The snail lives in Arctic waters as far south as the British Isles. It is found from the lower shore seaward, usually on seaweed.

Lacuna Periwinkle family
About 7 mm
Provinces: Arctic, Boreal
Named by Montagu in 1803

Common Wentletrap

Wentletraps get their name from a Dutch word meaning a spiral staircase. The tall, spire-like shell of the Common Wentletrap has whorls linked and braced by eight or nine strong axial ribs. Its colour is greyish-yellow, with brown spiral lines on the ribs. The animal, if you should be lucky enough to see it at low tide, is white with purplish-black specks. The snail lays its eggs in a string. It is common from intertidal sand flats into deep water. Its range is from Norway to the Black Sea.

Wentletrap family
About 4 cm long
Provinces: Boreal, Celtic, Lusitanian
Named by Linnaeus in 1758

Turton's Wentletrap

It is similar to the Common Wentletrap, but the whorls are more flat-sided. There are twelve to fifteen ribs on each whorl. It is usually darker in colour than the Common Wentletrap. It is moderately common on off-shore sandy bottoms. Its range is from Norway to Portugal.

Wentletrap family
About 4 cm long
Provinces: Boreal, Celtic, Lusitanian
Named by Turton in 1819

Common Pelican's Foot Shell

Three spines around the aperture make this shell look something like a bird's foot. It has a sharp spire whose whorls are decorated with ribs and knobs. It is a creamy tan in colour. It lives partly buried in mud off-shore, and is very common from Norway to the Mediterranean. You may find empty shells washed up on the beach. Worm-like animals sometimes make their homes in these shells.

Pelican Foot Shell family
About 3 cm long
Provinces: Boreal, Celtic, Lusitanian
Named by Linnaeus in 1758

Alder's Moon Snail

This moon snail has a small, globe-shaped shell, tan in colour with chestnut-brown streaks. The animal covers the shell with its foot. The forefoot, which it uses for digging, covers the short tentacles and eyes. It lives from intertidal sand flats to off-shore waters, feeding on tellins. Its range is from Norway south to the Mediterranean.

Moon Snail family
About 1.5 cm long
Provinces: Boreal, Celtic, Lusitanian
Named by Forbes in 1838

Arctic Trivia

Trivias have shells shaped like large, colourful tropical cowries. They are often called Groats or Nuns. The Arctic Trivia's shell is solid, with a long narrow aperture. Some animals live in the intertidal region and may be found in rock pools. Others live in deep water. The range is from Norway to the Mediterranean.

Trivia family
About 1.5 cm long
Provinces: Boreal, Celtic, Lusitanian
Named by Pulteney in 1799

Wooden Canoe-bubble

The shape, and the cream and brown or greenish colouring give this bubble shell its popular name. The animal is white to orange. It is a common species living just off-shore, feeding on small worms and bivalves. It ranges from the British Isles to the Mediterranean and the Canary islands.

Bubble Shell family – About 4.5 cm long
Provinces: Celtic, Lusitanian
Named by Linnaeus in 1758

Open Paper-bubble

The aperture of this snail is very large and wide, and the fragile, translucent shell seems to give little protection to the animal. In life, the pale-yellow mantle covers the shell completely. The snail protects itself by secreting a layer of sulphuric acid from its skin. It eats worms and small molluscs. It is common on sandy bottoms off-shore from Norway to the Mediterranean.

Bubble Shell family – About 4 cm long
Provinces: Boreal, Celtic, Lusitanian
Named by Linnaeus in 1767

Dillwyn's Necklace Shell

This necklace shell is found from Portugal south into the Mediterranean. It lives on sand just off-shore, from four to ten metres deep. The shell is a solid glossy tan, with chestnut brown markings. The over-layer is thin and yellowish-brown. It is also known as Dillwyn's Natica.

Moon Snail family – About 2 cm long
Province: Lusitanian
Named by Payraudeau in 1826

Fly-specked Necklace Shell

The not very complimentary popular name refers to the tiny light-brown spots that dot the creamy shell. It is also called the Fly-specked Natica and is a common shallow water Mediterranean species, seen in Italian fish markets. Its range extends to Portuguese waters.

Moon Snail family
About 5 cm long
Province: Lusitanian
Named by Gmelin in 1791

Spitzbergen Colus

This whelk has spindle-shaped shell, with a long spire. The whorls are well rounded, and have twelve to fourteen small, flat-topped spiral cords. The over-layer is reddish-brown. It is common off-shore in Arctic seas and near Scandinavia.

Whelk family
About 7.5 cm long
Provinces: Arctic, Boreal
Named by Reeve in 1855

Red Whelk

This is an edible whelk, common off-shore around the British Isles, Scandinavia and France. It has a large, strong shell, yellowish to grey. A rare all-white form occurs in the North Sea. Freaks may be found that are coiled left-handed.

Whelk family
Up to 20 cm long
Provinces: Boreal, Celtic
Named by Linnaeus in 1758

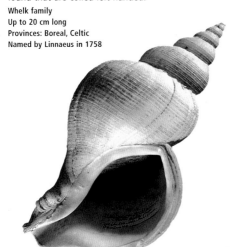

Contrary Neptune

This whelk is called 'contrary' because every specimen is coiled left-handed. The shell has well-rounded whorls and a pointed spire. The whorls are covered with weakly beaded cords. It is a rich, light-brown in colour, with a white aperture. The whelk is a moderately common off-shore species from Portugal south into the Mediterranean.

Whelk family
About 9 cm long
Province: Lusitanian
Named by Linnaeus in 1771

Mediterranean Bonnet

Bonnet shells are smaller relatives of the large, tropical helmet shells. Their name comes from their shape. The Mediterranean Bonnet's whorls have deep spiral grooves. The shell is cream with spiral rows of squarish, light-brown dots. The animal lives in shallow water. It is common in the Mediterranean and the Azores, and is more rarely found as far north as Portugal.

Bonnet Shell family – About 7.5 cm long
Province: Lusitanian
Named by Gmelin in 1791

Wrinkled Bonnet

Also called the Rugose Bonnet, this is the only
bonnet shell in British waters. It is common in the
Mediterranean. The shell is fairly thin but strong.
It has fine spiral threads, and a row of small round
knobs on the shoulder. The outside is creamy-brown
and the inside of the aperture is glossy white. It
lives off-shore on muddy bottoms.

Bonnet Shell family
About 6.5 cm long – Provinces: Celtic, Lusitanian
Named by Linnaeus in 1771

Attenuated Mangelia

'Attenuated' means stretched out or thin, and is a
good description of this little, slender shell. The
snail belongs to a large family with thousands of
species. It has a slit notch at the top of the outer lip
of the aperture, known as the 'turrid' notch. The
snail lives off-shore on sandy clay from Norway to
the Mediterranean.

Turrid family
About 1 cm long
Provinces: Boreal, Celtic, Lusitanian
Named by Montagu in 1803

Truncate Trophon

Deep grooves separate the
whorls of this shell, which are
strongly ribbed. The spire is sharp
and cone-shaped. The colour is a
yellowish-brown. This is a
common off-shore species in cold
water, occurring from Greenland
south to the Bay of Biscay.

Murex family
About 1.5 cm long
Provinces: Arctic, Boreal, Celtic
Named by Strom in 1768

Lamellose Coral Shell

'Lamellose' means covered with thin plates, and
refers to the busy but dainty sculpturing of this
coral shell. It is common in the Mediterranean.

Coral Shell family
About 2.5 cm long
Province: Lusitanian
Named by Calcara in 1845

Rustic Dove-shell

Dove-shells are aggressive carnivores, despite their small size. The Rustic Dove-shell has a spindle-shaped shell, white with brown or purple mottling. It lives on rocks on the lower shore and deeper, generally in large colonies. Its range is the Mediterranean and nearby Atlantic coasts.

Dove Shell family
About 3 cm long – Province: Lusitanian
Named by Linnaeus in 1758

Common Northern Whelk

This is the best known of the northern edible whelks, popularly known as a Buckie. It is a fierce predator, living off-shore in shallow water and also deeper. It has a solid shell, varying in colour from yellowish-brown to chalky grey. The shell is often covered with tiny barnacles. You may find a live specimen trapped in a rock pool near the low tide line. Its range is from Arctic waters to the British Isles.

Whelk family
About 7.5 cm long
Provinces: Arctic, Boreal
Named by Linnaeus in 1758

Atlantic Trumpet Triton

This large snail is a warm-sea dweller, and is found in the Mediterranean and the Atlantic Ocean. It has a tall, solid shell with heavy beaded sculpturing. The colour is a creamy white, with purple and brown markings. The interior is white, but the aperture is orange-pink.

Triton family
About 25 cm long
Province: Lusitanian
Named by Lamarck in 1816

Ovum Arctic Whelk

The name refers to the shell's shape, which is a cross between a spindle and an egg. It is smooth and creamy white, with convex whorls. The over-layer is very thin and translucent. It is common in the northern waters of Europe.

Whelk family
About 4 cm long – Province: Boreal
Named by Turton in 1825

Spotted Flask

This is the only European representative of a family of large carnivorous snails, most of which live in the tropics. They are called volutes, meaning spiral, because of the shape of their shells. The snail has an egg-shaped shell, thin but strong, with reddish-brown dots on a light-brown background. It is often dredged up from fairly deep water off Spain and Portugal.

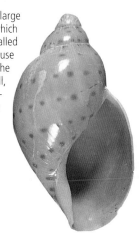

Volute family
About 6.5 cm long
Province: Lusitanian
Named by Gmelin in 1791

Greenish Admete

This carnivorous snail belongs to a family, the Nutmeg Shells, which are mostly found in warm tropical seas. The admete shells are a sub-family which prefer cold water. The Greenish Admete releases a greenish liquid when disturbed. It has a thin, spindle-shaped shell with beaded axial ribs. It is common off-shore in north-western Europe.

Nutmeg Shell family
About 2 cm long
Province: Boreal
Named by
Fabricius in 1780

Lathe Acteon

The Lathe Acteon is a pretty little bubble shell. It has a solid, spindle-shaped shell, with the aperture running three-quarters the length of the shell. It is pinkish-yellow, with three lighter spiral bands. It occurs off-shore from Iceland to Spain, and may sometimes be found on sandy beaches at low tide.

Bubble Shell family
About 1 cm long
Provinces: Boreal, Celtic
Named by Linnaeus in 1758

Northern Tusk

Tusk shells have tubular shells like miniature elephant tusks. They burrow into the sand head down, drawing in water through the other end, which projects above the surface of the sea-bed. The Entale Tusk mostly lives in deeper water, but in the north it is found in the intertidal zone. Its shell is ivory white, sometimes with a rusty stain on the narrow end. Its range is from Arctic waters south to Portugal. Shells are often washed up on shore.

Tusk Shell family
About 5 cm long
Provinces: Arctic, Boreal, Celtic, Lusitanian
Named by Linnaeus in 1758

Common Tusk

This is similar to the Entale Tusk, but is a truer white in colour, with yellowish-brown or pink tints towards the narrow end. The aperture at the other end is oblique, thin and jagged. It is common off-shore in muddy and sandy areas from southern England and Ireland southward into the Mediterranean.

Tusk Shell family
About 5 cm long
Provinces: Celtic, Lusitanian
Named by da Costa in 1778

Mottled Red Chiton

Chitons are called coat-of-mail shells, because their eight shelly plates look like armour. In shape they resemble woodlice. The plates are bound together by a leathery girdle, which is smooth in the Mottled Red Chiton. Its plates are rather sharply angular. Its name gives a clue to its colouring. The interior of the valves is rose-tinted. It is common off-shore from Norway to the British Isles.

Chiton family
About 2.5 cm long – Provinces: Boreal, Celtic
Named by Fabricius in 1780

Northern Red Chiton

This chiton has rather rounded plates, coloured light tan with orange-red markings. The interior of the valves is bright pink. The girdle is reddish-brown, covered with tiny scales. It is common off-shore on hard surfaces from Norway to Portugal.

Chiton family – About 2.5 cm long
Provinces: Boreal, Celtic, Lusitanian
Named by Linnaeus in 1767

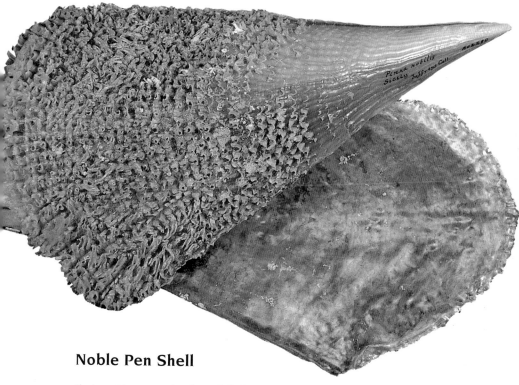

Pinna nobilis
Sicily 30 Jan 1980 Coll.

Noble Pen Shell

The largest known species of pen shell, the Noble
Pen Shell is like the Fragile Pen (see page 36), but
much longer. The outside of the shell is reddish-
brown, with overlapping scales. It lives in the
Mediterranean and south into the Atlantic Ocean,
in a similar way to the Fragile Pen Shell. Its golden
byssus threads have been used to make gloves
and socks.

Pen Shell family
Up to 1 m long,
but 50 cm more usual
Province: Lusitanian
Named by Linnaeus in 1758

Sulcate Nut-shell

'Sulcate' means marked with parallel grooves, and the shell of the Sulcate Nut-shell is a mass of fine radiating ribs and concentric growth lines, giving it a crisscross appearance. The outline is triangular, with the beaks off-centre. It has an olive-yellow over-layer with red patches. It lives off-shore on muddy bottoms, from Norway to the Mediterranean.

Nut Clam family
About 1.5 cm long – Provinces: Boreal, Celtic, Lusitanian
Named by Bronn in 1831

Common Nut-shell

Also known as the Nuclear Nut Clam, the Common Nut-shell is common off-shore from Norway to West Africa. It burrows into mud, sand or gravel. It has no siphons. It is a tiny bivalve, roughly triangular in outline. It never has radiating lines.

Nut Clam family
About 1 cm long
Provinces: Boreal, Celtic, Lusitanian
Named by Linnaeus in 1758

Turgid Nut-shell

Slightly larger than the Common Nut-shell, the Turgid Nut-shell is covered with very fine concentric lines, which on close examination prove to be beaded. It is greyish-white in colour, with a glossy, olive-yellow over-layer. It is common on sandy mud bottoms from Norway to the Mediterranean and West Africa.

Nut Clam family
About 1.2 cm long
Provinces: Boreal, Celtic, Lusitanian
Named by Leckenby & Marshall in 1875

Pitcher Nut-shell

The porcelain-like shell of this nut clam is elongated, with a pointed, somewhat upturned rear end. It is covered with fine, wavy concentric lines. The colour is greyish-white, matching the white sand in which it is commonly found. It ranges from Portugal to the Mediterranean.

Pointed Nut Clam family
About 1 cm long – Province: Lusitanian
Named by Linnaeus in 1758

Ark family – About 1 cm long
Provinces: Boreal, Celtic, Lusitanian
Named by Müller in 1776

Nodulose Ark

Sculpture of beading (nodules) covers the shell of this bivalve and gives it its common name. The shell is small, elongated and solid. The beaks are nearer the smaller front end. The gap for the byssus threads is very small. The shell is covered with a thin, light-brown over-layer. It is a common off-shore and deep water species, ranging from Norway to Portugal.

Dog Cockle

Also known as the European Bittersweet, this clam is almost circular in outline. The beaks are central. The colour is yellowish brown, with fine concentric and radiating lines. It is very common off-shore on sandy gravel from Norway to the Mediterranean and Canary Islands.

Bittersweet Clam family
About 6.5 cm long
Provinces: Boreal, Celtic, Lusitanian
Named by Linnaeus in 1758

Your Shell Collection

You should concentrate on collecting the shells of dead molluscs. You can study the live animals either on the beach or in an aquarium (see pages 38–9 and 44–5). However, collecting live molluscs is less likely to affect their survival rate than is usually the case. Many molluscs die young because they are eaten or because of changes to their habitat.

Labelling

When you have cleaned your shells, put them in little polythene trays (the sort that come with vegetables from the supermarket) or plastic boxes, and label each one. Very small shells can be kept in glass or plastic tubes, plugged with cotton.

Your label should give the popular name of the specimen, the scientific name if you know it, when and where you collected it, and any other important or interesting information.

Cleaning

When you take your shells home the first thing to do is to clean them. Most empty shells only need to be rinsed in clean cold water, and perhaps brushed over with an old toothbrush. Be very careful with more fragile shells.

If there is a crust or scale on a shell you can scrape and chip it away, but try not to remove any of the natural coating or weathering of the shell.

If you want to preserve the shell of a live specimen that has died, you will have to remove its soft parts. To do this, put the shell in a saucepan of cold water, bring it to the boil, and then boil it for about 10 minutes. Leave the saucepan to cool naturally, or you may damage the shell.

Or you can put the shell, inside a plastic bag, in the microwave oven. Set the oven on high for no more than two minutes for a 600 watt oven, or not more than two and a half minutes in a 500 watt oven. **Always ask permission before you use the stove, saucepans, or microwave oven.**

Equipment

This is the equipment you need to manage your collection, plus your field notebook and magnifying glass (see page 38):

1 **An old toothbrush** for cleaning specimens.
2 **A penknife** for cutting.
3 **A dental tool** to scrape away encrustations.
4 **A sharp point** for cleaning small holes. You can make this for yourself by mounting the pointed end of an old darning needle in a cork (for safety).
5 **Tweezers** for picking up and holding tiny shells.
6 **Cotton buds** for cleaning out shells.
7 **A short ruler** for checking the size of a shell.
Be careful with sharp tools.

A home for your collection

It's very easy to make some simple storage units to hold the shells in your collection. They needn't cost very much and you can add to them at any time.

All you need are some shoe boxes (with their lids) and some stiff card. If you don't have any shoe boxes at home, visit the local shoe shop and ask if you can have some of the ones that customers do not want. Then what you do is this:

1 **Measure the shoe box** across its short side and its depth. Draw a rectangle **(A)** on the card to match this size (eg 150 x 120 mm). Draw two lines across the rectangle to divide it into three.
2 **Measure the long side** (eg 300 x 120 mm). Draw another rectangle **(B)** to match this size. Draw two lines across it to divide it into three.
3 **Cut out each rectangle**; then cut another one each of **(B)** and **(A)**, using your first rectangles as your patterns. You could have extra partitions.
4 **Pad the bottom of the box** with cotton wool if you like. Then cut half way up each dividing line of each partition and slot them together as shown. Last, slide the partitions into the box.

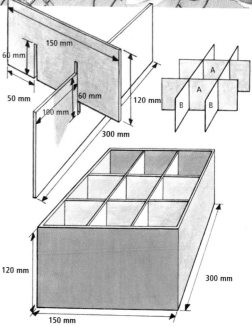

5 **Paint the boxes and their lids** with emulsion paint so that they match. Keep shells of the same family together and write their name on the short end or draw a picture of them there.

Small scale storage

You can use kitchen foil or cling-film boxes as storage for small shells.

1 **Measure the end of the box** (eg 50 x 50 mm) and draw a strip of these squares on some stiff card.
2 **Cut out the strip** and bend it into a series of right-angles as shown.
3 **Fit the bent card into the box** and glue the sides to the box.
4 **Pad the bottom** with cotton wool if you like and paint them to match.

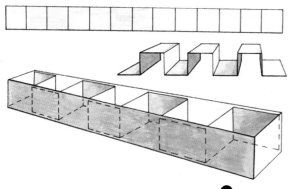

Great Scallop

This is one of the bivalves that is highly prized as food. It has a solid, almost circular shell, with two equal-sized ears. The right, or lower valve is reddish-brown, domed and overlaps the flat, left, or upper valve, which is white to cream. Young scallops attach themselves to rocks by a byssus thread. Older ones are free-floating. The scallop can swim by clapping its valves together. The Great Scallop is common in sandy areas off-shore from Norway south to Portugal.

Scallop family – About 10 cm long
Provinces: Boreal, Celtic, Lusitanian
Named by Linnaeus in 1758

Iceland Scallop

The Iceland Scallop's front ear is twice as long as the other, which helps to identify it. Its solid valves have about fifty coarse, irregular ribs. The colour is usually a dirty grey or cream. Some shells may be tinged with peach, yellow or purple. It is very common off-shore in Arctic seas, and is found from Iceland and Norway to the Shetland Islands.

Scallop family
About 7.5 cm long – Provinces: Arctic, Boreal
Named by Müller in 1776

Variable Scallop

This is a common shallow-water species, found under stones. The front ear is long, while the other one hardly exists. The valves have between twenty-five and thirty-five prominent ribs, bearing spines, and wavy edges. The colours of the valves vary, which is how it got its name.

Scallop family
About 6.5 cm long – Provinces: Celtic, Lusitanian
Named by Linnaeus in 1758

Kitten Scallop

The shell is small and fan-shaped, with the front ear about three times as long as the other. The colours and patterns vary, in shades of white, cream, grey, brown and purple. The number of ribs varies, up to about thirty. The ears have three to five little ribs. The scallop lives on sand and gravel from the low tide line downward. The range is from Iceland and Norway to Spain.

Scallop family
About 2.5 cm long – Provinces: Boreal, Celtic
Named by Müller in 1776

Queen Scallop

This is a common edible species, ranging from Norway to Portugal and into the Mediterranean. It lives off-shore on sandy or shelly bottoms. The valves are fan-shaped with ears of almost the same size. They have between nineteen and twenty-two rounded radial ribs, crossed by fine concentric lines. The background colour is yellow or white, with markings of red, pink, brown or purple. Its chief enemy is the starfish.

Scallop family – About 7.5 cm long
Provinces: Boreal, Celtic, Lusitanian
Named by Linnaeus in 1758

Hunchback Scallop

This is a common cold-water species, ranging from Norway to the Azores. It is the only scallop that cements itself by the lower valve to a rock or an old shell. The shape of this valve is irregular, and varies according to where the animal grows. The upper valve has about sixty prickly ribs. The colour is white, yellow, reddish or brownish.

Scallop family
About 4 cm long – Provinces: Boreal, Celtic, Lusitanian
Named by da Costa in 1778

Cat's Paw Scallop

This scallop has one ear much larger than the other. It has several large ribs, each sculptured with riblets. It is orange in colour. It lives off-shore and is common in the Mediterranean and off north-west Africa.

Scallop family
About 6 cm long
Province: Lusitanian
Named by Linnaeus
in 1758

Intetidal Rocks & Sand

Prickly Jingle Shell

Jingle shells are thin and semi-translucent, but remarkably strong. They are often washed up on beaches. The Prickly Jingle Shell is a common cold-water bivalve which attaches itself to rocks and other shells from the low tide line downward. It has an irregular shape, and the upper valve is rough, often with small prickles. The colour is a drab tan. Its range is from Iceland to France.

Jingle Shell family
About 2 cm long – Provinces: Boreal, Celtic
Named by Linnaeus in 1758

Round Doubletooth

This clam, also known as the Rotund Diplodont, belongs to a family that has two small teeth in each valve. These clams can build themselves nests. This clam has a solid shell with equal-sized valves. The colour is a dull white, with a light-yellow over-layer. There are fine concentric lines. The animal burrows into muddy sand, and is common from the British Isles to the Mediterranean.

Diplodont Clam family
About 2.5 cm long
Provinces: Celtic, Lusitanian
Named by Montagu in 1803

Gaping File Clam

Also known as Hians File Clam, this bivalve has a wide rear gape. It has a brown shell, thin but strong, and very obliquely elongated. There are about fifty small ribs. The animal has red-and-orange tentacles. This species is common from Norway as far south as the Azores.

File Clam family
About 4 cm long – Provinces: Boreal, Celtic, Lusitanian
Named by Gmelin in 1791

Northern Lucina

Also known as the Boreal Lucina, this bivalve belongs to a family of small clams with circular shells, somewhat compressed, and strong concentric ridges. In this species the ridges are sometimes worn away. The shell is white with a brown over-layer. The animal lives in sandy mud under shallow water. It has short siphons, and digs a tunnel in the mud with its foot for drawing in water. The range is from Norway to the Baltic and south to the Mediterranean.

Lucine Clam family
About 3 cm long – Provinces: Boreal, Celtic, Lusitanian
Named by Linnaeus in 1758

Grooved Astarte

Also known as the Sulcate Astarte, this clam belongs to a family of cold-water bivalves that live on silt or mud at moderate depths. The shells are sometimes washed ashore. The Grooved Astarte has an oval shell, slightly compressed. There are about twenty prominent, broad, concentric ribs, giving the bivalve its name. The colour varies from white to salmon-pink, with a light-brown over-layer. It is common off-shore from Greenland and Iceland to the Mediterranean.

Astarte Clam family
About 2.5 cm long
Provinces: Arctic, Boreal, Celtic, Lusitanian
Named by da Costa in 1778

Pellucid Razor Shell

This tiny razor shell has a brittle shell, rectangular in outline with both ends gaping. The colour is a dull white, with a yellowish-green over-layer. The animal lives in muddy sand off-shore, and is common from Norway to Portugal.

Razor Clam family
About 2.5 cm long – Provinces: Boreal, Celtic, Lusitanian
Named by Pennant in 1777

Grooved Razor Shell

A deep groove between the hinge and the front end identifies this bivalve, also called the European Razor Clam. The front end is obliquely cut off, the other end is rounded. The colour is yellowish with brown growth lines. The animal is found just off-shore, where it burrows into sand. It ranges from Norway into the Baltic Sea, and then south to the Mediterranean.

Razor Clam family
About 13 cm long
Provinces: Boreal, Celtic, Lusitanian
Named by Linnaeus in 1758

Intertidal Rocks & Sand

Heavy Egg Cockle

Sometimes called the Norwegian Cockle, this bivalve has a solid, almost smooth shell, with many very faint, little radial ribs. The colour is a dirty yellow, sometimes with red and brown markings. The over-layer is a thin greenish-yellow. This common species lives among broken shells and gravel from Norway to the Mediterranean and the Cape Verde Islands. It is called the Heavy Egg Cockle because it is more oval than other cockles.

Cockle family
About 7.5 cm long – Provinces: Boreal, Celtic, Lusitanian
Named by Gmelin in 1791

Cut Trough Shell

The other name for this bivalve is the Subtruncate Trough Clam. It is small, almost triangular, and much broader than long. There is sculpture of coarse concentric lines. The colour varies from greyish-white to brown. It lives off-shore on sand, and is very common from Norway to the Black Sea and the Canary Islands.

Trough Clam family
About 2.5 cm long
Provinces: Boreal, Celtic, Lusitanian
Named by da Costa in 1778

Thick Trough Shell

Another name for this bivalve is the Solid Trough Clam. It has a solid, smoothish shell of varying shape, but it is generally slightly longer than it is broad. It has central beaks. The colour is a whitish-grey, with a light-brown over-layer that is usually worn away. It is common on the lowest stretch of beaches, and in deeper water, from Finland to Morocco. Empty shells are often washed ashore.

Trough Clam family
About 4 cm long – Provinces: Boreal, Celtic, Lusitanian
Named by Linnaeus in 1758

Poorly-ribbed Cockle

The small number of ribs on its shell give this cockle its name. It is common in intertidal and off-shore sand in the Mediterranean and Black Sea, and off West Africa. Its northern limit is the southern coast of Brittany, in France, but a few live in Mont St Michel Bay in northern Brittany.

Cockle family
About 5 cm long – Provinces: Celtic, Lusitanian
Named by Sowerby in 1839

Oblong Otter Shell

This is similar to the Common Otter Shell, but longer, and with a characteristic concavity on the hinge side. The beaks are close to the front end, while the over-layer is dark brown. This is a common shallow-water clam, ranging from the British Isles to the Mediterranean.

Trough Clam family
About 15 cm long
Provinces: Celtic, Lusitanian
Named by da Costa in 1778

Elliptical Trough Shell

The shell is an almost perfect ellipse in outline. The front end is more rounded, and the beaks are located in the centre. The shell is small and nearly smooth. The colour is tan, with a smooth, shiny brown over-layer. The interior of the shell is a glossy white. It is common in muddy sand and fine gravel from the Arctic to the English Channel.

Trough Clam family
About 2.5 cm long
Provinces: Arctic, Boreal, Celtic
Named by Brown in 1827

Common Otter Shell

Also known as the European Otter Clam, this bivalve has a large, long shell. The shell gapes widely at both ends to allow for the animal's massive frontal siphons. The colour is yellowish-brown with a thin, olive-brown over-layer, but may be pink. It is common from just off-shore into deeper water, ranging from Norway and the Baltic Sea to the Mediterranean and West Africa.

Trough Clam family
About 13 cm long
Provinces: Boreal, Celtic, Lusitanian
Named by Linnaeus in 1758

Intertidal Rocks & Sand

Story Tellin

The tellins are a group of bivalves that suck up tiny bits of food from the sea-bed. This tiny shell is an elongated oval, with the rear end pointed and twisted to the right. The colour is white, but may be tinged with yellow or orange. The over-layer is yellowish. It is common in off-shore sand from Norway to the Black Sea and north-west Africa.

Tellin family – About 2 cm long
Provinces: Boreal, Celtic, Lusitanian
Named by Gmelin in 1791

Blunt Tellin

This bivalve is sometimes called the Thick Tellin. It is circular in outline, with the beaks almost in the centre. There is sculpture of concentric ridges, with fine radiating lines showing between them. The colour is a dirty tan, and the beaks are tinged with orange or pink radial rays. It is common off-shore from Norway to West Africa.

Tellin family – About 6.5 cm long
Provinces: Boreal, Celtic, Lusitanian
Named by Pennant in 1777

Thin Tellin

This is a very common little bivalve over most of its range, which is from Norway to north-west Africa. However, it is scarce in the Mediterranean. It sucks up food debris with a long inlet siphon. The shell is delicate and shiny, white tinged with pink, sometimes tinged with violet or yellow. Empty valves are often held together by the ligament, and look like little butterflies.

Tellin family – About 1.8 cm long
Provinces: Boreal, Celtic, Lusitanian
Named by da Costa in 1778

Faroes Sunset Shell

As its name implies, this bivalve is more common in the north of its range, which is off-shore from Norway and the Faroe Islands to West Africa. The shell is elongated and almost oblong. The rear end is narrower, and has a rounded keel. The surface is covered with crowded concentric ridges. The colour varies from brownish-pink to purple. There are darker radiating rays.

Sunset Clam family
About 5 cm long – Provinces: Boreal, Celtic, Lusitanian
Named by Gmelin in 1791

Heart Shell

This bivalve is also known as the Oxheart Clam. The beaks are curled over toward each other, and when seen from the side with the two valves together it is distinctly heart-shaped. The shell is globular, with no gape. The colour is tan, sometimes with reddish streaks, and the over-layer is greenish-brown. The animal is as much sought after for food as its shell is prized by collectors. It is a common off-shore species ranging from Iceland and Norway to the Mediterranean.

Oxheart Clam family – About 7.5 cm long
Provinces: Boreal, Celtic, Lusitanian
Named by Linnaeus in 1758

Chamber Venus

Venus clams live just a little way below the surface of the sand, mostly off-shore, though some are found above the low tide line. Shells are frequently washed ashore. The shell of the Chamber Venus has many raised concentric ridges, which make it easy to identify. The colour is a whitish-tan, sometimes with reddish-brown rays. It is common from Norway to West Africa.

Venus Clam family – About 5 cm long
Provinces: Boreal, Celtic, Lusitanian
Named by Linnaeus in 1758

Intertidal Rocks & Sand

Smooth Artemis

Also called the Wolf Dosinia, this clam has a solid shell, circular in outline. The beaks are forward of the mid-line. There is sculpture of fine concentric ridges, crossed by faint radiating lines. The shell has a yellowish over-layer. The animal lives in sand and silty mud off-shore, and is common from Iceland to the Mediterranean.

Venus Clam family – About 4 cm long
Provinces: Arctic, Boreal, Celtic, Lusitanian
Named by Poli in 1791

Rayed Artemis

Another name for this clam is the Mature Dosinia. It has a circular shell, flatter than that of the Smooth Artemis, and less glossy. The colour is light-brown, with reddish-brown rays running from the beaks to the margin. It lives in sand from the intertidal zone downward. It has a wide range, from Norway to Portugal, the Mediterranean and the West African coast.

Venus Clam family
About 5 cm long – Provinces: Boreal, Celtic, Lusitanian
Named by Linnaeus in 1758

Common Pandora's Box Shell

Pandora was the first woman, according to Greek mythology. She opened a box entrusted to her and let out all the evils of the world. The Common Pandora clam has a thin, box-like shell, the right valve flat and the left valve convex. The exterior is chalky white with a thin grey over-layer. The interior is pearly white. It is common off-shore from England to the Mediterranean and the Canary Islands.

Pandora Clam family – About 2.5 cm long
Provinces: Celtic, Lusitanian
Named by Linnaeus in 1758

Arctic Saxicave

If you see a pair of red-rimmed holes in a soft rock on the shore, they are the ends of the siphons of an Arctic Saxicave. It is a small clam, which either nestles in rock crevices or bores into the rock. Its shell is oblong, chalky white and usually misshapen. It is common on the lower shore and below the low tide line from Arctic Seas through Norway to the Mediterranean and the Azores.

Saxicave Clam family
About 5 cm long – Provinces: Arctic, Boreal, Celtic, Lusitanian
Named by Linnaeus in 1767

Blunt Gaper

Another name is the Truncate Soft Shell Clam.
It is used as seafood. The animal burrows in
sand from the middle shore downward. It has
an elliptical shell, abruptly cut off at the rear end.
The colour is a dirty white. This is a common
Arctic species, found from the North Sea south
to the Mediterranean.

Soft Shell Clam family
About 6.5 cm long
Provinces: Arctic, Boreal, Celtic, Lusitanian
Named by Linnaeus in 1758

Convex Thracia

Thracia clams are cold-water bivalves, with white,
porcelain-like shells. The shell of this species is an
elongated oval, rather plump, with the right valve
larger and more domed than the left valve. The
beaks are near the centre, and that of the left valve
sits in a hole in the beak of the right valve. The
colour is white to green, and the over-layer is a
greenish-yellow. The animal lives in sandy mud
off-shore from the Norwegian Sea south to the
Mediterranean.

Thracia Clam family – About 5 cm long
Provinces: Boreal, Celtic, Lusitanian
Named by Wood in 1815

Youthful Thracia

This bivalve is found on sand in shallow water from
the British Isles to the Mediterranean and the
Canary Islands. Its shell is an oval oblong, strong
but brittle. There is sculpture of uneven concentric
lines. It is white or cream in colour, with a light-
yellow over-layer.

Thracia Clam family
About 7 cm long
Provinces: Celtic, Lusitanian
Named by Pulteney in 1799

Things To Make

Shells make excellent decorations. Some of the large shells are ornaments on their own, but many small shells can be used to decorate other objects.

Decorate with shells

The best way to attach the shells is to put a layer of modelling clay or Polyfilla over the object you wish to decorate – for example, a box, a bottle or vase. Press the shells into the clay to make a pattern, using shells of different sizes and colours. After the clay dries out, you can coat your decorated object with varnish to protect it and give it a glossy finish.

Wreath of shells

This is a good way of displaying your shells and also makes an unusual present.

1 **Take a generous handful of straw** and twist it into a 'snake'.
2 **Wind fine wire tightly around it** to hold the straw together and make it tight and firm.
3 **Bring the two ends of your snake together** and overlap them. It will help if the ends are thinner than the rest of the snake. The wire will then bind the snake into a ring.

4 **You can attach the shells** to the ring with wire or pins, but it is better to stick them on with a quick-drying glue.

Jewellery from the sea

Small shells make beautiful and unusual jewellery. Why not make yourself a pendant or a brooch?

1 **Buy a bell mount and ring** from your local craft or hobby shop and some PVA glue.
2 **Choose a fine example of a shell** and wash it carefully in warm soapy water and leave it to dry.

Birds and monsters

Use two different mollusc shells, glued together, to make a series of exotic birds. Add a small feather to form the tail and make them more lifelike.

You can also invent your own creatures by sticking together shells to make monsters. Don't stick more than two shells together at a time and let them dry before adding more. Here are some ideas to start you off.

3 **Glue the bell mount to the top** of your shell and leave it to dry.
4 **Thread the ring through** the bell mount and pinch the ring tight (you may need help for this). Thread the pendant on to a ribbon or chain.

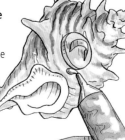

5 **For a brooch**, glue the mount to the side of the shell next to the opening as shown.

6 **To make the shells shine**, you can paint a coat of varnish over them.

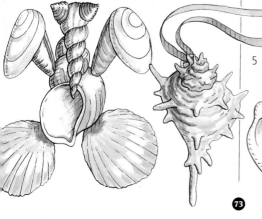

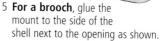

Wood & Rock Borers

On the windswept, wave-lashed shore many animals seek shelter. Some, such as mussels, anchor themselves to rocks with byssus threads. Limpets cling like suction cups. Many bivalves burrow into the sand or mud of the beach or the sea bottom. One group, however, takes shelter in the rock itself, not just in cracks and crevices, but by boring holes in which to hide.

The Arctic Saxicave (see page 70) sometimes seeks shelter in this way. However, there are a number of species which always bore holes for shelter, leaving apparently hard rocks looking like a sponge. Sandstone, limestone and hard clay are all treated in this way. Some species bore their holes partly by chemical action, others drill out their holes just by rubbing their shells backwards and forwards.

The so-called shipworms are not worms at all, though they have long bodies like earthworms. They are bivalves, but with greatly reduced shells that do not enclose more than a fraction of the animals' bodies. In the days of wooden ships they were a very real menace to shipping.

Living animals are common in floating logs, wharf pilings and other underwater timbers. As it grows, a shipworm burrows into the wood, leaving behind it a long tunnel connected to the open sea. The animal grips the inside of the tunnel with its foot, and twists its valves to and fro to wear away the timber. It absorbs food from the sea water, which it takes in through a siphon that sticks out of its hole, but the worm can also digest some of the cellulose from the timber.

Gould's Shipworm

There are a number of species of shipworms in European waters, and only experts, using scientific books on the subject, can identify them. Gould's Shipworm is a typical example. As the picture shows, the damage caused by shipworms is immense. As in all species, the siphons can be withdrawn, and the hole is then closed by a pair of feathery, limy plates called pallets.

Shipworm family
About 20 cm long
Provinces: Boreal, Celtic, Lusitanian
Named by Bartsch in 1908

Wood & Rock Borers

European Date Mussel

As its name suggests, this shell is shaped like a large date, with the beaks at the narrow front end. The outside is light brown with fine growth lines. The inside of the shell is bluish-white. The animal bores into limestone and coral skeletons in shallow water, using an acid to dissolve the rock, and then cutting into it with its valves. It also bores into wood. Its range is from Portugal into the Mediterranean as far east as the Adriatic Sea.

Mussel family
About 7 cm long – Province: Lusitanian
Named by Linnaeus in 1758

Rock-eater Clam

This animal bores into soft, chalky rock. It has a thick shell, with valves longer than they are wide. The shell has sculpture of coarse, wavy radial ribs. It is moderately common from the English Channel south into the Mediterranean and the Black Sea. It was accidentally introduced into the northern part of its range about 1890, when British oyster beds were restocked from Portuguese beds.

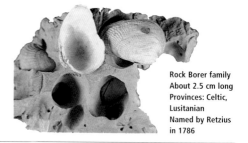

Rock Borer family
About 2.5 cm long
Provinces: Celtic,
Lusitanian
Named by Retzius
in 1786

American Piddock

Also called the False Angel Wing, this animal is not a true piddock, but is closely related to the Rock-eater Clam. It has an elongated, chalky white shell, which is rather fragile. When the two valves are seen edge-on, they look rather like stage angel's wings. The shell has many radial ribs, those in the front being larger, with prominent scales. The species was accidentally introduced into Europe with American oysters. It bores into clay and peat, and rarely into soft limestone.

Rock-borer family – About 5 cm long
Province: Celtic – Named by Lamarck in 1818

Common Piddock

This large borer is also found on the east coast of America, where it is called the European Piddock. It bores into peat, wood, sandstone and shale, and can excavate a gallery up to thirty centimetres long. The shell is long and brittle, gaping at both ends. The beaks are close to the front end. The front end of the shell has about forty spined, radiating ribs. The rest of the shell has concentric ridges. The animal ranges from Norway to the Black Sea, and is common locally.

Piddock family
About 13 cm long
Provinces: Boreal, Celtic, Lusitanian
Named by Linnaeus in 1758

Striate Martesia

This is an American species of piddock, which has been accidentally introduced into British waters. The shell varies in shape, but is usually pear-shaped. It is white, with a tan over-layer. It bores into wood.

Piddock family
About 2.5 cm long
Province: Celtic
Named by Linnaeus in 1758

Paper Piddock

This little piddock is common in clay, peat and sandstone on the coasts of the British Isles and France. It has a frail, elongated oval shell. The shell has a wide gap at the rear end with a serrated edge.

Piddock family
About 2.5 cm long
Province: Celtic
Named by Turton in 1819

Find Out Some More

Useful organizations

The best organization for you to get in touch with is your local Country Wildlife Trust. There are forty-seven of these trusts in Great Britain and you should contact them if you want to know about wildlife and nature reserves in your area. Ask your local library for their address, or contact:

The Wildlife Trusts (formerly Royal Society for Nature Conservation), The Kiln, Waterside, Mather Road, Newark, Nottinghamshire NG24 1WT (01636 677711).

Wildlife Watch is the junior branch of The Wildlife Trusts. Local Wildlife Watch groups run meetings all over the country. Again you can find out about your nearest Wildlife Watch group by contacting The Wildlife Trusts.

The Conchology Society of Great Britain & Ireland, 35 Bartelmy Road, Newbury, Berkshire. RG14 6LD They hold a meeting with a talk in the Natural History Museum, Exhibition Road, London SW1 on the third Saturday afternoon of October to May each year and have field meetings across the country from June to September. Members are encouraged to bring shells to these meetings. They also have many foreign members, so you might be able to arrange to swop shells with someone in Australia or the USA. There is an annual subscription.

Marine Conservation Society, 9 Gloucester Road, Ross-on-Wye HR9 5BU (01989 566017). This charity campaigns for clean seas and beaches, and against the trade in rare shells and sea creatures. They work in conjunction with WATCH. They also produce Fact Sheets on habitats, marine animals and pollution, costing 50p each.

National Trust for Places of Historic Interest or Natural Beauty, 36 Queen Anne's Gate, London SW1H 9AS (020 7222 9251). For membership and enquiries: The National Trust, PO Box 39, Bromley, Kent BR1 3XL (0870 458 4000). They own more than 232,000 hectares of countryside throughout England, Wales and Northern Ireland. These include many woods, nature reserves and sites of special scientific interest. Most are open to visitors, but you usually have to pay to get in. The National Trust also run courses with school groups; ask your teacher to find out about these.

In Scotland, contact the Head of Education, **The National Trust for Scotland**, Wemyss House, 28 Charlotte Square, Edinburgh EH2 4ET (0131 243 9300).

Useful books

European Seashells Guido Poppe & Yoshihiro Goto (Verlag Christa Hemmen, Grillparzerstrasse 22, D-6200 Wiesbaden, Germany, 1991). Three volumes, written in English.

Illustrated Guide to the British Coast (Reader's Digest, 1991) An illustrated guide book and atlas giving useful information about the part of the coast nearest to you.

The Macdonald Encyclopedia of Shells (Macdonald & Co, 1979).

Seashore Life of Britain & Ireland Bob Gibbons (New Holland Publishers, 1991).

Young Naturalist at the Seashore Ken Hoy (World International Publishing, 1990).

Collins Pocket Guide to the Seashore of Britain and Northern Europe Hayward, Nelson-Smith and Shields (Collins, 1996)

Collins Handguide to the Sea Coast Ovenden and Barrett (Collins, 1981)

Index & Glossary

Places to visit

There are over 14,400 km of coastline around Britain. Almost anywhere you go, you will find shells on the beaches. In Europe, the Algarve in Portugal is a good place for shells. The North Sea beaches of Holland and Germany are another good hunting ground.
Rocky pools and shores: Sheringham, Norfolk; Filey Brigg, N. Humberside; Boulmer Haven, Northumbria; Great Cumbrae Island, nr Largs, Strathclyde; **Sand or mud flats:** Shell Bay, Studland Heath, Dorset; The Wash, Lincs; Red Rocks, West Kirby, Merseyside; Morecambe Bay, Lancs; **Estuaries and lagoons:** Chesil Beach, Dorset; River Orwell, nr Ipswich, Suffolk; Cemlyn, nr Amlwch, Gwynedd; River Humber, Humberside; Solway Firth, Dumfries & Galloway; **Intertidal rocks and sand:** Purbeck Marine Wildlife Reserve, Dorset; Oxwich, nr Swansea, W. Glamorgan; Isle of Tyree, Strathclyde; **Borers:** Borth submerged forest, Dyfi National Nature Reserve, nr Aberystwyth, Dyfed.

Index & Glossary